Praise fc
WANDER W

T0372426

"Intensely practical and surprisingly philosophical, this book is the ideal companion for the solo traveler, both before and during her trip."
—Pauline Frommer, co-president of FrommerMedia and editorial director of Frommer's Guidebooks

"Not only does Beth Santos pour her extensive knowledge of travel into *Wander Woman's* pages, but she peppers the text with personal stories pulled from her own travels and her journey in launching Wanderful. *Wander Woman* has a lot of soul: it marries the practical and inspirational, leaving readers with a treasure trove of thoughtful tips that truly cover all aspects of the solo travel experience. As Santos writes herself, this is the book every woman should read before traveling alone."
—Nikki Vargas, author of the bestselling memoir *Call You When I Land* and *Wanderess*, and senior editor of *Fodor's Travel*

"Like a good friend who comforts and nudges you past your comfort zone, *Wander Woman* will certainly become your new BFF and help you achieve your solo travel dreams. Wherever you are in the process of planning your trip, this is the book you'll want to guide and ground your journeys both closer to home and farther away. Beth Santos is a travel industry gem, skillfully weaving together both experience and empathy on every page. She encourages us to open our hearts, minds, and cultural perspectives as we explore our own neighborhoods with a fresh lens or land up on the other side of the world. An engaging invitation to all women to wander and to wander well, *Wander Woman* is destined to become a classic."
—Dr. Anu Taranath, professor, racial equity consultant, and author of *Beyond Guilt Trips: Mindful Travel in an Unequal World*

"This book is a trailblazer, changing the narrative we've been told about traveling solo as women. I've always traveled with others—with my family, girlfriends, or colleagues, but *Wander Woman* has inspired me to explore the world on my own!"

—Fran Hauser, bestselling author of *The Myth of the Nice Girl* and *Embrace the Work, Love Your Career*

"*Wander Woman* is a book for every traveling woman no matter where she is on her journey. Reading the book was like revisiting my own journey and remembering those moments that made me truly who I am today. Before I even started reading the book tears streamed down my face, because the manifesto is so POWERFUL. Beth exposed the parts that nobody sees or speaks about. 'Solo doesn't mean single' and 'Alone, but not lonely,' are hands down my favorite sections. Traveling solo has been one of the best things I've ever done and is where I truly found ME. I'm excited for other women to take that journey of self-discovery through travel because of the connection they make to this book."

—Martinique Lewis, award-winning diversity in travel consultant, president of the Black Travel Alliance

"As a woman devoutly addicted to music-swelling-movie-moment-travel-magic, I appreciated this inspiring book's advice about how to navigate the quieter, less perfect moments of solo travel—and the permission to forgive myself when I stumble."

—Kristin Newman, author of *What I Was Doing While You Were Breeding: A Memoir*

"*Wander Woman* is a revelatory guide to living your life on another level, forever changed by the world around you. Filled with real-world examples and practical tips to get you out of dreaming and into action, Beth has written a reassuring, unflinching road map for every traveler. Whether it's your first time eating a meal alone or your fiftieth time around the world, *Wander Woman* is a must-read."

—Juliana Dever, actor and founder of
CleverDever Adventures

"Whether a seasoned solo traveler or stepping out solo for the first time, Santos's warm engaging prose feels like travel counseling. Written in an accessible conversational style, it feels like listening to your most trusted friend empowering you to see the world; urging you to bask in the unique magic and transformational experiences that only solo travel can provide."

—Lola Akinmade Åkerström, internationally bestselling and
award-winning author of *Due North*

"Come one, come all—*Wander Woman* is a treasure for anyone looking to travel more or get more out of their travels. With a grounded yet optimistic approach, Santos helps open the door to the most important place for any traveler or wannabe traveler—their mind. Once that happens, every other door is that much easier to swing open with confidence. P.S.: The resource section at the back of this book is worth the cost of entry…and then some."

—Steph Jagger, traveler and author of *Unbound: A Story
of Snow and Self-Discovery* and *Everything Left to
Remember: My Mother, Our Memories, and
a Journey Through the Rocky Mountains*

"*Wander Woman* is a remarkable guide tailored for the adventurous spirit of women travelers. In this empowering book, Beth masterfully weaves together personal anecdotes, practical tips, and cultural insights to inspire and embolden every woman seeking to reclaim her space in the world. Most importantly, Beth's book celebrates the countless voices, stories, and unique perspectives of diverse travelers who are often forgotten in travel narratives. This is a must-read for every woman ready to embark on her own journey of self-discovery, empowerment, and wanderlust."

—Tue Le, CEO of Remote Year

"In this heartfelt, thoughtful, and inspiring book, Beth beautifully captures what it means to travel. She empowers us to embrace the vastness of the world, explore with an open-mind, and walk into the world with confidence, care, and a sense of humor. Whether you've never traveled alone before or are an experienced solo traveler, this book will break down barriers and inspire you to book your next flight with your best friend—yourself."

—Lillian Rafson, founder of Pack Up + Go

"As a sustainable travel expert who exists to try and help people travel better, I'm always over the moon when trusted industry voices express why it matters so much with such intelligent yet easy-to-follow advice. Beth inspires and guides with honesty and conviction in a way that makes you wonder how any reader could travel any way but better after reading her book!"

—Juliet Kinsman, sustainability editor of *Condé Nast Traveler*

WANDER WOMAN

How to Reclaim Your Space,
Find Your Voice, and Travel the World, Solo

BETH SANTOS

balance

Balance
Hachette Book Group
1290 Avenue of the Americas
New York, NY 10104
GCP-Balance.com
Twitter.com/GCPBalance
Instagram.com/GCPBalance

First Edition: March 2024

Balance is an imprint of Grand Central Publishing. The Balance name and logo are trademarks of Hachette Book Group, Inc.

The publisher is not responsible for websites (or their content) that are not owned by the publisher.

The Hachette Speakers Bureau provides a wide range of authors for speaking events. To find out more, go to hachettespeakersbureau.com or email HachetteSpeakers@hbgusa.com.

Balance books may be purchased in bulk for business, educational, or promotional use. For information, please contact your local bookseller or the Hachette Book Group Special Markets Department at special.markets@hbgusa.com.

Library of Congress Cataloging-in-Publication Data
Names: Santos, Beth, author.
Title: Wander woman : how to reclaim your space, find your voice, and
    travel the world, solo / Beth Santos.
Description: First edition. | New York : Balance, [2024]
Identifiers: LCCN 2023046037 | ISBN 9781538741313 (trade paperback) | ISBN
    9781538741320 (ebook)
Subjects: LCSH: Women—Travel—Handbooks, manuals, etc. | Middle-aged
    women—Travel—Handbooks, manuals, etc. | Older women—Travel—Handbooks,
    manuals, etc. | Women travelers—Handbooks, manuals, etc. | Travel—Safety
    measures.
Classification: LCC G156.5.W66 S26 2024 | DDC 910.2/020844—dc23/eng/20231023
LC record available at https://lccn.loc.gov/2023046037

ISBNs: 9781538741313 (trade paperback); 9781538741320 (ebook)

Printed in the United States of America

LSC-C

Printing 1, 2023

For Nora and Zoey

"Actually, the best gift you could have given her was a lifetime of adventures."

—Lewis Carroll, Alice in Wonderland

CONTENTS

Contents

WANDERFUL MANIFESTO

I am a trailblazer,
An adventurer,
An explorer,
A traveler.
I want to see the world
Whether I am loaded with suitcases
Or carry only what's on my back.
I travel because it teaches me as much about the world
As it does about myself.
I am curious.
Resilient.
Powerful.
Compassionate.
I want to live a life in which my friendships span continents,
Where I can cherish our differences
And embrace our similarities
Not because I have read about them
But because I have lived them.
I am a daughter,
A neighbor,

A mother,
A sister.
I travel with my friends,
My partner,
My kids,
And sometimes I travel on my own.
My life is too short to be stagnant.
I ignore the people who doubt me
I pave my own path
I dream big
I conquer mountains
And sometimes I am shaken to my core.
I believe in a global sisterhood of women
Who help me see myself for who I am
And challenge me to be who I want to be.
I am Wanderful.

—Wanderful manifesto, created 2017

SO, YOU WANT TO TRAVEL

"Life is either a daring adventure, or nothing."
—Helen Keller

I F YOU HAD TOLD ME BACK IN 2009 WHEN I TOOK ONE OF MY first solo trips that women were the majority of travelers and commanding 80 to 85 percent of consumer travel decisions,[1] or that women had been traveling alone and (mostly) successfully since AD 400,[2] I wouldn't have believed you. How could I? I was living overseas in a small country called São Tomé and Príncipe, a two-island nation off the coast of Gabon in West Africa. I would wake up in the morning and sweep tiny crabs out of my bathroom that had crawled into the house from the ocean while I was sleeping. I would ride my motorcycle to school past the amused shouts of neighbors teasing me with the town joke that I was the lone female motorcycle taxi driver (truth be told, I could barely start and stop the thing, let alone carry another person with me). I was one of four known Americans living in the country at the time, and while I was immersed in new information about other people's worldviews, I was still trying to identify my own.

Living abroad was an amazing experience; it was also lonely. I didn't fit conventional expectations of women where I was living, especially in how I dressed, how I acted, and how I spent my time, so I didn't have a lot of female friends. It was one of the first times I had realized how different women's experiences abroad actually were, and when I say "different" I don't necessarily mean different from men's, or even different from our experiences in our home countries; I mean different from *every other place* we visit as women. Each place we go has a new set of structural norms, cultural nuances, and gender expectations that we must adapt to and learn.

In São Tomé I was filled with so many complex, conflicting emotions. The strange power dynamics I felt as a twenty-three-year-old white woman who led an entire program at a school for Black children with little credentialed teaching experience (and the mixed feelings that plague me about that even today when I look back). The unfamiliar gender norms that surrounded me, and the fact that most of my colleagues were male. The hilarious yet common experiences of trying to acquire sanitary products (or, let's be honest, condoms) at the local pharmacy.

There were plenty of books and TV shows about travel, but when you flipped on the Travel Channel it was mostly the faces of white men that dominated the screens: Rick Steves or Anthony Bourdain. When I could find anything online about women's experiences abroad, it was often surface-level content related to fashion or shopping, or scary, fearmongering content about how dangerous it was to be a woman traveling alone. I never saw myself in those images or stories.

So it was in my bedroom in São Tomé, listening to the sound of the ocean literally steps from my window, that I started to write a blog. I shared my own experiences of traveling as a woman. And then I searched for other women who wanted to do the same.

The stories I curated became an online magazine, filled with women's words about their own realities. They wrote about how it felt being a Colombian woman who was considered white at home and brown in the States. They wrote about the uncomfortable experience of being trans and going through airport security. They wrote about the endless search for thigh chafing creams so that they could travel comfortably, and the aggressive daily reminder that the world wasn't built for—or even moderately welcoming of—plus-size women.

Those stories grew into Wanderful, a company I founded in 2013 that has blossomed into a sisterhood of travel lovers who want to help and guide one another, a network for thousands of travel content creators and entrepreneurs, and an advocate for a better and more inclusive travel industry. It became not just about sharing travel tips but about creating a space where women who see travel as a core part of their identity could be unequivocally themselves. It became my baby—my life's work, in so many ways.

But this book isn't about Wanderful. This book is about you. It's about the fact that you are about to go on a trip, or you're thinking about traveling alone at some point. Maybe you've told someone you want to do it. Maybe that intention is still sitting inside you, peeking out like a crocus in the snow, not even whispered out loud yet. Or maybe you've done it sixteen times already but haven't had the words or the concepts to really examine it in all its layers. For those of you who are just starting to stretch your travel legs, this book is for you. It's the book that I wish someone had written for me when I started traveling. The words that no one seems to have written yet, but desperately need to be said, for women who travel alone. And fear not, travel veterans—this book is for you, too. For you to rethink the ways that you've traveled and rethink the messages that you send to your fellow women about what travel should be. To refine your existing skill set and to find new ways to embrace this place we all call home, a world that can do better by all of us. While this book speaks most directly to new travelers, I believe all travelers will find something new here.

I'd like to think that the only thing we have to do is convince ourselves to travel, and we'll have a magical and wondrous experience. It would be really amazing if the world worked that way. Unfortunately, many of us as women find ourselves on an uphill battle, from dealing with the instant concern that flashes across the faces of our family and friends when we first voice the desire to travel alone, to navigating the diverse realities of womanhood and the other intersections of our identity while overseas.

I have yet to meet a solo woman traveler* who hasn't experienced some sort of microaggression either before or during her trip. Sometimes it's hidden behind a mask of concern from a friend or family member who simply wants you to be safe.

---

* While not always grammatically the most correct, we'll use the word "woman" in place of "female" in various instances, like "solo woman traveler" instead of "solo female traveler" in order to recognize and create space for both cis and trans women in this book, though I hope all genders can enjoy many of its more universal lessons.

Other times it comes from the kind concierge at the hotel who asks if you're sure you need only one hotel room key, or the person on the bus who asks if you're saving a seat for your husband. Or it could even be from the friends and colleagues overseas who joke that you must be the female motorcycle taxi driver, and can they have a ride? While at surface level these comments seem harmless, they add to the narrative that women can't and shouldn't travel alone, and when paired with some of the outright aggressive shaming that we see in the media, they can set our travel plans awry—or cause us to back out entirely.

But I promise, it doesn't have to be that way.

WHAT IS YOUR REASON FOR TRAVEL?

In my experience, all travels begin with an intention, whether we're conscious of it or not. Sometimes you feel the need to get out or to move forward, and before your mind has a chance to catch up, you're in a car four hours down the nearest freeway. Other times, we travel because we come from a place of curiosity, wanting to know more about the rest of the world that may have felt distant from us. We travel to escape; we travel to lean in; we travel for work; we travel to connect to ourselves. It's not the same for all of us, nor must it be just one thing. But getting clear on which direction you're leaning—your *why* for travel—can be a compass rose for your journeys ahead. It can give you direction, and focus, in your wayfinding.

Maybe you've always wanted to travel. Maybe you have an opportunity that you didn't have before. Maybe someone you know got back from an amazing trip and it has piqued your interest. Maybe you've always been curious. Maybe you want to see the world but are sick of waiting for friends or family or a partner to get on board.

Maybe you're not sure what you're doing, or where you're going, or exactly how you're doing it. Maybe you're in the process of healing from something or grieving someone. Maybe you're looking for a new place to start.

Through the Wanderful community and my own travels I've met thousands of fellow travelers, both experienced and new. I've gotten to know some exceptionally well, and others just in passing. And while their reasons for travel are different, there is one thing that rings true for all of us, and that's this: We expect *a lot* from our travels.

In just about every travel book and movie, travel changes the characters on an almost cosmic level. The travel photos that make up our social media scroll appear to be nothing short of enlightening. When we go into a travel experience, we think we already know what it should feel like and how we should come out of it completely transformed, because we feel like we've seen it already documented in front of us.

We have thoughts, whether conscious or not, about who travel is for—about who can and should travel the world, and who can and should do it alone. About what they should look like. And we have a lot of limiting beliefs about what travel itself should be like—what constitutes "real" travel and what doesn't. How much money we need to do it. How adventurous we need to be, how far we need to go, and how many passport stamps we need to have in order to be legitimate.

But these myths hold us back. They keep us from exploring and growing. They stifle our unique voices and experiences, because they make us sound fake if we're not complying with them. They make us fearful about what could happen to us abroad, preventing us from digesting any real information and putting the onus on us as women to protect ourselves or to just stay home.

We are made to believe that women traveling solo are a niche, a small segment of people who don't travel a lot; an exception to a rule.

But we're not a niche, and we're not an exception. We are the rule itself.

WHAT THIS BOOK WILL (AND WON'T) DO

If you picked up this book hoping for a step-by-step guide to sell all your belongings and eat pizza in Naples or hike the famed Pacific Crest Trail (PCT), I'm sorry to disappoint you. That's not this book. Travel is so much bigger than the logistics or destination, so let's set some ground rules:

This book *will not* give you a comprehensive list of travel safety products and scare you out of doing anything by yourself because you're alone and vulnerable.

This book *will not* turn you into a travel packing superstar and teach you how to fit a month's worth of clothing into a fanny pack.

This book *will not* blind you with the belief that everything is going to be perfect and rose-colored and wonderful. (Spoiler alert: If you're having a delightful and seamless time all the time during your trip, it means that you're not challenging yourself enough.)

This book *is not* your travel guide to specific exotic and famous locales, a budget planner, or a memoir.

Instead, we're going to reground in that travel mindset and

learn to reclaim our space in the world, together. By the end of this book, I want you to have the skills and confidence you need to take on the world, one trip at a time.

So we're going to talk through the hard stuff. We're going to bust myths about what society has told you your entire life about who should travel solo, and why, and how.

You're going to meet some amazing people who are challenging the narratives about solo travel and advocating for a more inclusive and equitable travel industry.

You're going to learn about your responsibility as a traveler and the complicated feelings you'll ultimately have if and when you immerse yourself in someone's home and worldview.

We're also going to talk about fear—not because it doesn't exist, but because it's very real and because it needs to be dealt with, and because it's complicated. Safety is a more complex issue than you may think.

And we're going to talk about how and when travel is very different for women—from understanding gender norms in a new place, to dealing with street harassment, to getting a grip on sexism and chauvinism when paired with the complications of a new culture and geography.

And, yes, we'll also learn some basic tips and tricks for defining personal safety, eating alone, what to pack, structuring an itinerary, how to get that trip off the starting blocks, and what to do after you come back.

This is the book that I hope every woman receives before she travels alone. I hope it gives you the language to think about and process your travels, but also gives you the freedom to continue to explore these concepts even long after you've returned home and throughout the journey of your life.

And I hope this book inspires you—to get out to see the world, to be fearless, to manage your mistakes along the way, to be a true Wander Woman, and to feel confident in giving yourself this time in a world where women are still told that doing things for themselves is selfish and irresponsible.

To that I say, let the adventure begin.

Part One

LET'S BUST SOME TRAVEL MYTHS (NO EXPLOSIVES REQUIRED)

Chapter 1

TRAVEL IS A MINDSET, NOT AN ITINERARY

"Adventure can be an end in itself.
Self-discovery is the secret ingredient."

—Grace Lichtenstein

"HAVE YOU EVER TRAVELED SOLO BEFORE?"
I've posed this question countless times to people at Wanderful meetups and travel shows. It seems like a simple question, but the answer is always much more complicated. It's usually preceded by hesitation and a moment of reflection.

"Well, yes," they'll say. "But it was only for a business trip" (as if the reason for travel affects whether you're alone or not).

Or "Yes, but only because my friend dropped out at the last minute, and I didn't want to cancel my flight" (as if doing it out of necessity rather than choice disqualifies you).

Or "Yes, but only for a weekend" or "only on a road trip" or "only in a town that was a ninety-minute drive from my house" (as if all of these reasons mean that you can't actually claim your solo travel cred).

We have a lot of expectations about what solo travel should be. We think that in order for travel to be considered truly "solo," the traveler needs to be alone all the time, for days (maybe even weeks!) on end. She must be sitting on the cliff of a mountain, reflecting on her place in the world or on a quest for self-discovery. She has to be the mistress of selfies and requesting tables for one. We put these expectations on ourselves as much as we put them on one another, constantly forcing our own interpretations of what solo travel *should* be into other people's experiences and realities, which in turn makes us self-conscious about if we've actually experienced the "real thing" or not.

But let me tell you something: It's *all* real.

In fact, before I take the time to introduce you to some of the neat ways to travel solo, I think we need to address an important myth about the many expectations we have about what solo travel is and what it looks like. Let's call this Myth #1: "Your trip does not need to look like Instagram."

INSTAGRAM DOESN'T DECIDE IF YOUR TRIP "COUNTS"

What does a solo trip look like?

Take a moment to flip over to your social media channel of choice—Instagram, or Facebook, or even TikTok, or just about anywhere—and have a look at some of the popular travel content. Go ahead, do it now. We'll have a little exercise together.

What do you see?

Sweeping landscapes?

Someone standing at the top of a mountain looking fierce?

A meal to die for?

A perfectly sun-kissed young person roaming through the winding streets of Italy?

Thin white women wearing large hats and laughing as they look back over their shoulders?

Lush gardens?

Color filters and sparkles that make everything look just... Sigh. Perfect?

I won't say that social media is the cause of all of our problems, but I will say that social media is partially to blame. We experience FOMO (fear of missing out) when we see others doing really cool stuff, and social media allows us to see lots and lots of people doing really cool stuff in five minutes, curating the best of everyone's lives and leaving out all the moments we are watching Netflix or eating dinner with our family or studying.

Of course, we are partly to blame for these lies, too. We post perfectly produced pieces of content on social media because we really hate to show each other our flaws. We *want* our travels to look perfect, because we want to show others that we know what we're doing, that we don't make mistakes, and that we're having The Best Time™. And it's not just the editing and the filters—it's about deciding what photos we're going to take (and post) in the first place.

The media that's served to us (online, but also on TV, in movies, magazines, even stock photos on well-intentioned websites) often leads us to believe that travel wholly consists of mouthwatering meals eaten behind secret waterfalls; or empty, picturesque cobblestone alleys exploding with flowers; or spontaneous colorful weddings that you get invited to by your airplane seatmate. We believe so much in these exceptional travel experiences that we start to expect them as everyday travel interactions. But unlike our actual travels, these expectations get the added benefit of perfect photography, professional lighting equipment, a few minutes of Photoshop, and some creative storytelling. As a result, when we think about our own solo travel hopes, we discount anything that doesn't fully look that way, not giving a chance to the actual adventures waiting for us. The expectations have become so strong at points that we have felt cheated if we *don't* have something remarkable happen to us; or if it rains; or if we eat a meal that's just "average."

Experienced travelers know that the real adventures aren't always precisely about what happens *to* us, but rather about how we digest and perceive what we experience and what we take from those lessons. However our travels manifest themselves, whether we're keeping tight on a budget, staying close to home, going for only a few days, tacking them on to another trip, or doing a RTW (round-the-world) sojourn, each type of travel can look and feel very unique. But they're all real and legitimate. The point that ties all of these types of solo travel together is that you're taking the trip for *you*. Everything else that makes your trip what it is has to do directly with the mindset you have.

RECIPE FOR A TRAVEL MINDSET

If you saw the word "mindset" and it immediately sent you into a state of alarm ("Oh, this is one of *those* books? But all I wanted to do was learn how to travel!"), don't panic. I'm not going to launch you down a rabbit hole of self-discovery (well, not yet anyway) or make us do trust falls together. You will actually learn tips and tricks to make your adventures easier, safer, and more meaningful. But before we can go there, I want to take a minute to talk about the most important thing you'll take with you on any trip: your perspective.

Somewhere along the way, we started to equate "travel" with going really far away, ideally on a plane, to have thrilling adventures and eat delicious things. But the more I've traveled, the more I've realized that while these experiences do deliver many of the feels that we crave when we travel, it's not actually the itinerary that creates the travel experience at all.

In fact, in order to have a truly transformative travel experience, you need to do only three things:

1. **Challenge your preconceptions.** Put yourself in a position of questioning what you know and have learned up to this point, and be willing to look at something differently.
2. **Try something new.** Whether it's new tastes, sounds, sights, or a combination, commit to experiencing something you haven't experienced before.
3. **Get uncomfortable.** Willingly embrace the unfamiliar, step outside your comfort zone, and lean into the things that are different or curious to you.

It might seem strange to you to see travel defined not as an act of going from place to place but as a series of experiences that you yourself go through mentally and emotionally, but at the end of the day that's what it is. Traveling farther away might facilitate some of this (after all, it's inevitable that you'll try something new or get uncomfortable when you're in a place you've never been before), but it's not necessary.

From here on out, I want to challenge you to think of travel differently: not in terms of miles, or points, or passport stamps, but in terms of how much you learn, how far you step outside of your comfort zone, and how much you allow that trip to fundamentally change you.

The joy of broadening the definition of travel is that it opens ways to have transformative, exciting, novel experiences close to home. It's an equalizer. And some of those assumptions we carry that travel has to be astronomically expensive, or take a lot of vacation time, or always require a passport, suddenly aren't true. So, with our new mindset in hand, let's get some of our facts straight.

FACT: YOU DON'T HAVE TO SPEND A LOT OF MONEY

I want to be clear: Traveling *is* an enormous financial privilege. The cost is one of the biggest reasons many people don't travel in the first place.[1] Travel may feel completely off-limits for some, and it *is* completely off-limits for others. It is expensive, even if you're coming from a rich country. And it takes time, which many people don't have, especially if you're working two or three jobs at once; or caring for children, an aging parent, a friend, or someone else who needs you.

On a global scale, even being able to consider going on a trip puts you in the upper echelon of financial privilege. According to the World Bank, nearly half of the world struggles to meet basic needs every day; 3.4 billion people live on less than $5.50 a day.[2] For those people, travel is not just unaffordable; it's impossible. Our economy already draws a line in the sand between the "visitors" (those of us who have the opportunity to travel) and the "visited" (those of us who don't). This was seen in a new light during the COVID-19 pandemic, when borders were shut for the unvaccinated, creating a rift between travelers with easy access to the vaccine and those whose countries' structural systems, logistics, and infrastructure made it impossible to access (as of April 2022, the entire continent of Africa was still only 12 percent vaccinated against COVID).[3] Exercising our privilege to travel comes with the responsibility to make sure we are entering others' home countries and cities consciously and thoughtfully. Unfortunately, we don't always do that. We'll discuss that a bit later.

But, for those of us for whom travel *is* a possibility, it also doesn't have to be a luxurious, "stay every night at the White Lotus" free-for-all. In fact, for some people, it's cheaper to travel than it is to pay rent at home, simply because the cost of living around the world is different. Even if that's not you, remember that you can still have wonderful, life-changing solo travel experiences while staying with a friend and shopping for meals at the local grocery store. You don't need to be dining out, or splurging on attractions, in order for that trip to "count." You just need to be there and to be present for whatever moment you're in.

In the early days of my career, I worked for an international nonprofit called Rotary, based just outside of Chicago. I thought I was an experienced traveler until I met my friend Jessica, another junior staffer. It seemed like every couple of weeks she was off on another trip, and it wasn't just to Michigan or Wisconsin—it was to Colombia, or the Republic of Türkiye, or Malaysia. I couldn't understand how she traveled to all of these distant places on her nonprofit salary. I knew how much money she made. It was the same amount that I made. It wasn't much. So at one point, I just flat-out asked her how she did it.

"Well," she replied, matter-of-factly, "I think about where I want to go, and then I just eat ramen noodles until I've saved up my grocery money."

Today, Jessica is the international expat and creator behind @FroOnTheGo and has spent years traveling the world while teaching abroad. I think a lot about Jessica's story when I think of financial privilege, because even as an entry-level employee, she defied a lot of really big assumptions that we set up for ourselves. You might think that you can't travel because it's too expensive, but what exactly does travel mean to you? If it means staying in five-star resorts and dining out every meal and flying first class with limo airport transfers, you're right—it's expensive, and probably too expensive for a lot of us. But there are lots of other ways to travel as well. Hostels provide a safe way for people to explore the world on a budget; opportunities like WWOOF allow you to work on a farm in exchange for room and board. You can volunteer or teach abroad to earn free lodging or an income. While I wouldn't recommend the nutritional consequences that come with a diet based on prepackaged ramen noodles (and I doubt Jessica would either), the point is that you don't always need a hefty disposable income to see the world. Your creativity can take you far.

Better still, knowing that travel is first and foremost a mindset, it's possible to travel in your own backyard. You can find ways to get uncomfortable, try new things, and embrace discomfort just as easily on a road trip or a day hike you've never done before. Which brings us to our next point…

FACT: YOU DON'T HAVE TO TRAVEL FAR

How far, exactly, does someone need to travel in order for it to "count"? Do you have to take a flight? What about a car? Do you have to cross a border, or speak a different language, or get a passport stamp? Is someone a "better" traveler than someone else simply because they have set foot in more places around the world, even if not a single one of those places had any meaningful effect on them?

And while we're at it, how long do you have to travel, anyway? A month? A week? Thirty-six hours? If you live in El Paso, Texas, but cross the border to Mexico for one hour, does that count? What if it's a six-hour layover in Amsterdam? What if it's an afternoon detour off the New Jersey Turnpike? Does that somehow feel like less of a travel adventure?

One of the biggest myths perpetuated out there is that the quality of a trip is directly related to how long you're gone or how far you go. To be truly traveling, we think we need to traverse thousands of miles, or be away for a long period of time (or at least our entire two weeks of paid vacation, where we cram every little thing in and get home exhausted and needing a whole other vacation to recover).

Our world is full of magnificent travel experiences. Rather than thinking about how far you need to travel in order for that trip to "count," I want you to ask yourself: *How* close *can I travel while still stepping outside my comfort zone and learning new things?*

Can you do that an hour away from home? Half an hour? How about in a five-minute walk? When you think about being fundamentally challenged just five minutes from home, you start to think about travel not as something that happens *to* you but as a change that you invite by taking the time to really notice and understand the world around you and the people, cultures, and experiences that are different for you. That is the magic of having a travel mindset, something we'll talk more about in part 2 of this book.

FACT: SOLO DOESN'T MEAN SOLITARY

In the mid-1840s, a man by the name of Henry David Thoreau decided to move to the woods of Massachusetts for two years, two months, and two days of isolation. He lived in a tiny cottage that he built himself on the shores of Walden Pond, keeping at least a mile of distance between himself and the rest of society. That experience became *Walden*, one of America's most famous transcendentalist books today.

For many, the idea of solo travel brings on similar Thoreau-induced visions of complete isolation, far from any sign of humanity. Maybe somewhere you have conjured up images of traveling alone in a similar way.

Like this one: You're sitting on a mountain somewhere, peering into the valleys below, a bag of trail mix in your hand. "It's just me and you, pal—all these months," you say to your trusted golden retriever as you pull out a box of matches to light a fire.

Or maybe you're driving a convertible along the empty California coastline, the sun setting in the distance. The ends of your yellow silk scarf flap in the wind while you adjust your big Hollywood sunglasses and laugh lightheartedly to yourself (actually, this story is even more absurd than it seems, as I have yet to know a part of California that isn't riddled with traffic these days).

Maybe you're envisioning yourself as that mysterious, sexy

Carmen Sandiego type, glass of Malbec in hand while sitting confidently at the bar, a solitary creature chatting with the bartender with such flair that the people around you wonder if you're an expat, or even—dare I suggest—a local!

If you've gone solo before, maybe your vision is not so pristine; maybe you're sitting by yourself in that same busy restaurant but instead of having sashayed in wearing a bright red coat and sexy boots, you're slightly disheveled with sneakers that are a dead giveaway of your foreigner status, only worsened by the fact that your server has asked you for the third time if you're being joined by someone else because they keep forgetting that you're alone. You chuckle nervously, knowing that you're taking up valuable table space and feeling about as helpful as a sack of potatoes.

There are a lot of different ways to experience solo travel, and it doesn't mean that you have to hike the PCT or renovate a Tuscan villa by yourself. You might not even feel very brave or confident about it, and you know what? You don't have to feel brave to do it.

Your solo travel experience could look like signing up for a group trip (on your own), or taking a class (with other people), or staying in a hostel (with other guests). It might be a short moment by yourself, enjoying a bite to eat in a restaurant you've never ventured to before, or arriving a few days early before a conference. The amount you decide to interact with others, or even rely on others, is entirely up to you. Suggesting that it wasn't "the real thing" because of the length of time you spent away, or the distance covered, only robs you of the potential to build confidence in yourself, learn to enjoy your own company, and celebrate your adventures.

FACT: IT DOESN'T ALWAYS GO PERFECTLY

Here is one promise I can make for you right now: Something WILL go wrong on your trip.

Yup, sorry to burst your bubble, but it's going to happen. You're ready to check into your hotel only to realize that they don't have your name on their guest list. Or you get lost trying to navigate the city bus system and realize you've been riding in the opposite direction for the last twenty minutes. Or you think you're ordering a salad and get presented with some slimy tongue-looking thing.

If this is your first time traveling, some of these occurrences might throw you off. It can feel scary when things go wrong, because you don't have a fallback—another person whose trusty navigation skills can get you back on track or a friend with whom you can have a chuckle over your misfortune. You might not find it easy to communicate what you need and thus solve your own problems. But that's exactly what practice is for.

Just because it wasn't perfect doesn't mean you didn't go solo, or that it wasn't worthwhile, or that it didn't "count" as travel. In fact, it's totally the opposite! This is how you grow— proof that you made it, you did it, and you have new capacity to do it again. In time, I promise, you'll learn to embrace the challenges. You'll have a copy of your hotel registration confirmation and realize that they actually did have your reservation but just switched your first and last names. You'll find a local who speaks a little English who can help you hop off the city bus and catch the one going the other way. You'll laugh at yourself for ordering the slimy tongue thing and then discover it's actually delicious (or maybe you'll just have a snack later).

Some of the best parts of travel are the misadventures. They make the greatest stories (and memories—don't forget the old adage "You'll laugh about this later!"). They also teach you a lot. With each misadventure, you'll get savvier. You'll know how to prepare, and you'll also learn that no matter how prepared you are, you'll still have challenges (which, once you're a seasoned traveler, you'll take in stride).

It's what you learn about yourself and your world during these travels that makes all the difference.

FACT: YOU CAN BE A TOURIST *AND* A TRAVELER

Our expectations about solo travel are closely tied to deeply held expectations about what constitutes "real" and "authentic" travel in the first place, beyond just the length and the destination of your trip.

How many times have you seen the statement "Be a traveler, not a tourist" proudly displayed on a website or a bumper sticker? I, for one, used that phrase all the time. I thought that finding the "hidden gem" restaurants where the locals ate or avoiding the popular attractions (read: "tourist traps") of a region or negotiating a killer deal at a local market qualified me as a bona fide traveler.

There are important reasons why you might want to support local businesses while traveling or avoid overcrowded and over-touristed areas as a way to help preserve the historical and environmental integrity of a place. But I'm not talking about that. I'm talking about passing judgment on someone's travel choices because they're not "adventurous" or "unique" enough.

Rather than thinking about travel as something you *do* (either well or poorly), I want you to start thinking about travel as something you *exercise*. As a muscle that can be developed and toned. And just as the size and strength of our muscles are different, our travel skills also evolve and mature on their own scale. Some of us have traveled a lot, resulting in some pretty big travel muscles. Others who haven't had as much of a chance to travel might feel that burn of exercise a little bit more quickly. But the discomfort isn't for nothing—it just means your muscles are getting stronger.

While running a marathon or climbing a major rock face will certainly help you build muscle faster, you don't always need to do a body-crushing workout to get healthier. In fact, sometimes you can do it with a couple of cans of corn and a VHS of Richard Simmons in your living room. Building your travel muscle is like that, too.

Travel is personal, and none of our travel muscles are built or toned in quite the same way. Some of us work those muscles more than others do. What matters is that you are stepping outside of *your* comfort zone, not someone else's. There is a lot of shaming that goes on between travelers, but I want to say loud and clear that having more passport stamps does not make you a better person than anyone else. Pooh-poohing someone's trip to Paris because they spent their whole time visiting all the tourist attractions and not "living life like a local" is a quick way to get uninvited from the next dinner party. You're not a better person just because you can bench-press three hundred pounds. What's important is that we're all at the gym in the first place.

Whether you plan to jet-set around the world or drive across the state, the most valuable thing you can do is embrace your travel mindset and dive into the experience at hand. So much can be learned from every experience; so many lessons can be taken away from even the smallest of things. It doesn't happen only when you're sleeping between sheets of the highest thread count or with a view of the Pyramids of Giza outside your window. It happens when you're sitting at that little mom-and-pop café that didn't have a single Yelp review, which you stumbled into desperate for Wi-Fi. It happens in the busy energy of your hostel kitchen while you're making hummus because you can't for the life of you find anything halal around here. It happens on long, boring bus rides. But only if you embrace your situation and dive in.

Your travels are real. Wherever you go, for however long, in whatever way, they're legitimate. And so are you.

Chapter 2

EVERYBODY—AND EVERY BODY—TRAVELS

"Your journey is worthy and incomparable."

—Marlene Valle

It's 2014 and I'm sitting in a carpeted gray room, a large microphone positioned in front of me. I've got these enormous headphones over my ears, drowning out any external noise. Inside, I'm listening to the sweet butter sound of the host of a weekend radio show on Chicago's public radio station, WBEZ 91.5 FM.

I've been invited onto the show to talk about Wanderful, which at this point has grown from a cutesy travel blog that I started in 2009 into a full-fledged business that I incorporated in the last year with a mission of connecting and supporting women travelers. The host introduces me. He's got salt-and-pepper hair and sits relaxed in a polo. We're seated next to each other at a long, curved table, microphones hanging over us with pop filters positioned in front of them. "So, Beth," he says in that sweet, sweet radio voice, "women in travel, huh? Is there a market for that?"

I was floored. But if you're like most people, you're probably at this point not thinking anything about the question that the radio host just asked: "Women in travel? Is there a market for that?"

Lucky for you, you're reading this book, and you're about to get enlightened.

You're going to be so enlightened that by the end of this chapter you're going to be clawing the back of your chair just to get the word out. You're going to call the next Top 40 radio station and instead of asking for another play of "My Heart Will Go On" (sorry; that was a millennial joke), you're going to slightly aggressively yell, "Did you know that women dominate the travel industry but most don't even know it?" and trust me, when you know all of this information, you won't be able to stop there.

Welcome to a Brief History of Women's Travel 101. I'm your instructor, Beth. Sit down; get your pen out. Actually, don't get your pen out. Just keep reading.

Let me try to explain to you the reason why, to me, this question is so fundamentally angering, so ridiculously frustrating.

Imagine that, instead of me sitting at a radio station, it's Bill Gates sitting in that exact same chair. He owns Microsoft, whose operating system, Windows, holds 70 percent of the global desktop PC market.[1]

We've established that Bill Gates is a big deal (like that needed to be established). Now imagine he's sitting in that chair and the radio host says, "So...Windows. Is that a thing?"

I mean literally, today, in contemporary times, imagine

a radio host asking Bill Gates if Windows is a cute emerging niche of the tech industry.

It's almost impossible to comprehend a world where someone asks Bill Gates this question. Do they have no sense whatsoever of what the market looks like?

But that's exactly how I feel about the women's travel market or what many people like to refer to as the "women's travel *niche*."

To date, women make 80 to 85 percent[2] of consumer decisions in the travel industry.

No, I didn't say 8 percent. I said *80 to 85* percent.

Yes, at least *80 percent of the time* when someone is booking airfare, deciding on the destination of a family vacation, or reserving a room block for a corporate event, that someone is a woman.

In some ways this is because of who is at the helm of booking trips. In the US workforce, women still make up 89 percent of receptionists and 93 percent of administrative assistants.[3] As a married mom of three, I make nearly all of our travel decisions for my family, which means I'm deciding the travel fates of five people every time we step out into the world.

It's women who are driving the purchasing decisions of the entire travel industry. Add to that the fact that we're also traveling more. Two-thirds of all solo travelers identify as women. Some companies report numbers as high as 85 percent.[4] So we're traveling more than anyone else, *and* we're picking the itinerary. Yet, as a society, we don't often speak to women as the real loci of that power. In fact, we don't speak to women at all. That's why we call women in travel a "niche."

Remember how in chapter 1 we noticed the ways the media

shaped our expectations of what travel should be like? Well, it also shapes our understanding of who gets to do it, what they look like, and the identities they hold. The media tells us that the real travelers are conventionally attractive, scruffy-bearded older (but not too old) white men with sun-kissed skin taking us into hidden temples and tiny eateries. When women get the spotlight, they're skinny, white, underdressed cis women, usually sitting on top of a mountain somewhere or brazenly navigating an oceanside highway with a giant paper map while their legs dangle out the side of the car (assumedly because they're not driving). If they're older than forty, they're usually "still-attractive" recent divorcées (though, let's be real, I'll happily get down with a glass of wine and a screening of *Under the Tuscan Sun* pretty much anytime). If they're people of color, they're more likely to be represented as the local who's being visited, or the hospitality employee, rather than the traveler who's getting out there.

But here's the thing: We—the people who are doing the traveling, the people making the vast majority of consumer decisions, the people who are taking the solo travel movement by storm— are endlessly diverse. In 2018, 28 percent of the journeys taken by Muslim women were solo.[5] The average age of a solo traveler in the UK was fifty-seven in 2017.[6] In 2019, 13 percent of American travelers were Black.[7] One stock photo does not define all of us. We as women cannot, and will not, be overlooked. Because when we are, a self-perpetuating cycle keeps us from exploring our world. We know because it's happened for generations.

INTRODUCING THE MYTHICAL NORM

Here's a good term to add to your literary tool belt: the "mythical norm." Coined by the great writer, feminist, and civil rights activist Audre Lorde in 1984 (and introduced to me by the incredibly insightful and brilliant author Dr. Anu Taranath, whose book *Beyond Guilt Trips: Mindful Travel in an Unequal World* will completely change the way you think about your travels), the mythical norm is the perception that white, thin, male, young, heterosexual, Christian, and financially secure men are "normal"—and anyone else is, well, not. Unfortunately, a lot of these descriptors could also be used to paint the picture of a modern-day solo traveler.

The more we consider people who match that description to be "normal," the more we see ourselves as *abnormal*, or "other." Exceptions to a rule. It isn't necessarily bad to be abnormal, but it does affect how you think about yourself in relation to the rest of the world. Your challenges feel bigger, because the odds are stacked against you. You suddenly have more to overcome. And that feels pretty overwhelming.

It's one thing to feel abnormal; like an outlier. It's a whole other thing for the entire rest of society to believe that you are abnormal. Reputable journalists ask questions like "Is solo female travel a niche?" because we've been conditioned to think we are a niche. Being unaccustomed to images of plus-size women traveling, brown women traveling, queer and trans women traveling, and disabled women traveling (and, by the way, traveling happily of our own volition, not because we were left at an altar somewhere or a friend canceled a trip on us at the last minute) means that when people who look this way *do* travel, they strike up a curiosity in others, whether in real life or on social media. It worries our friends and family, who maybe want us to see the world, but also don't want us to experience the challenges that may come with being "the first." Our whole society becomes

33

altogether unprepared to see any woman traveling alone who doesn't match their initial expectations. And when they are confronted with the reality of what we actually look like, that cognitive dissonance catalyzes an unpleasant knee-jerk reaction.

The biggest issue, of course, is that this perception of diverse women traveling alone being "abnormal" will further continue in cycles for as long as we let it. Generations of women will follow after you having to deal with the same bullsh*t that you did. We will continue to be pushed down, ignored, blocked, judged, harassed, gaslighted, mansplained to, whistled at— because we stand out from what people expect in travelers; because people don't realize how many of us there are; because the status quo simply never changed.

YOU SHOULD BE SEEN—AND CELEBRATED

When we believe that solo travel is only for some of us, we hold on to expectations that our trips will look the same as everyone else's. We ignore, or perhaps forget, the fact that solo travel looks and feels different for everyone, because we all go into our solo travels with different backstories, personalities, and levels of experience.

When you travel the world alone, your entire identity—who you are, what you look like, what you believe in—comes with you. At times, that identity is challenged. You might stick out more because you don't look or sound or act like most people at your destination. You might experience certain expectations or preconceptions being completely questioned (it might even be you who begins to question them). But suggesting that a solo travel experience is the same for everyone, and failing to share stories of travelers outside this narrow definition, leads us to believe that travel truly *is* the same for all of us. That's how we begin to construct painful and overtly general narratives about solo travel being either rosy and perfect or perilous and dangerous, regardless of who we are or where we come from. "There's a very real harm that can and does happen when people do not see themselves made real and where other people do not acknowledge, or really think of, or know about their existence," said Jumoke Abdullahi, cofounder of the Triple Cripples, a platform by and for women, femmes, and non-binary people of color living with disabilities.

The bottom line is that women are traveling more than ever, and they are much more diverse than you think. They're old; they're young. They're brown, disabled, straight, gay, trans, plus-size, blind, neurodiverse. They wear hijabs, or itty-bitty bikinis, or babies on their backs. When we fail to celebrate our diversity, we perpetuate the idea that we're abnormal and allow discrimination and prejudice to seem justified, which can result in meaningful impacts on our health, safety, and self-esteem—not to mention the stifling of innovation in the industry. We should no longer view these identifiers as deviations from the norm or exceptions to a rule. Our diversity is the very rule itself. That diversity should be talked about, highlighted, considered, and celebrated. It should be embedded in the fabric of our travel experiences. We should be seen in all of our differences.

If we sit back and let the old men in the boardroom continue to make decisions for us, we can't expect the next generation of travelers' experiences to look much different from ours. Luckily, there are some pretty incredible movements headed by brilliant people who are working to challenge these narratives and advocate for a more inclusive travel equation, and they're doing that by creating spaces and building communities where people across different intersections feel seen and supported. These initiatives not only tell us that we all have unique qualities that make us different from one another, but also affirm that each of those qualities belongs in this world. They teach us important lessons about the challenges that remain while showing us how we can find ways to overcome them anyway. I'd like to introduce you to a few of them right here.

YOUR BODY BELONGS IN THE WORLD

Somehow, I managed to travel to Brazil without bringing a swimsuit.

Yes, it's on the packing list of just about every reasonable person who would ever visit Rio de Janeiro. Some might put it right up there with a toothbrush. But I didn't.

It's hard to remember why. Did I intentionally leave it behind? It wouldn't have been unlike me. There were moments in my life when I pretty much avoided swimsuits at all costs, preferring to hang out on the beach in shorts and a tank top because the idea of giving someone permission to gaze at every unforgiving inch of my body felt uncomfortable, offensive even.

But Rio broke me. Walking along Copacabana Beach, the sun hot on my shoulders, the wind whipping through my hair, I knew the only thing I had left to do was spend a day in the sand—and a really cute swimsuit was going to be part of that.

When you decide to buy a swimsuit in Rio, it's not hard to find a place to shop. I poked my head into the first beach cabana I saw, which was lined with racks of colorful bikinis. But colorful is a gross understatement. These bikinis were neon green, fluorescent yellow, hot pink. Some were polka-dot, some bedazzled in rhinestones, and others were made of fabric with a glitter sheen. Some had bra tops so small I wondered how they got any sort of nipple coverage. And. Every. Single. Swimsuit. Was a G-string.

I peeked back outside the tent with new eyes. Everyone on the beach was wearing the tiniest bikini I had ever seen. I would say they made a simple one-piece look like something your grandma would wear, but that would be a lie because grandmothers were wearing G-strings, too. Imagine a beach filled with the ittiest, bittiest bikinis, and they're dressing pretty much every body out there. Old bodies. Young, lean bodies. Voluptuous, curvy bodies. Bodies with scars and cellulite and wrinkles, completely exposed for the world to see.

That moment blew my mind and has stayed with me all these years. Growing up in American culture, I was taught certain lessons that I didn't realize until then. That women's bodies were made to be gawked at. That only certain bodies "could" wear certain swimsuits. That anyone outside that norm was at best unusual, at worst inappropriate. That we should judge others—and ourselves—harshly.

The messages that many women have been told from childhood—that our bodies should fit into a singular type and if they're different, they're wrong—aren't too far off the messages that most women are told about who can travel, whether explicitly or implicitly. We are told that only certain bodies can and should travel. That anyone with a body outside standard definition should pay more or be okay with a slower, uncomfortable work-around. That any body outside of the mythical norm will just have to cope on the sidelines.

If you don't know what I mean, take a minute to search You-Tube for animator Stacy Bias's viral video, *Flying While Fat*, created in 2016. In it, you experience a firsthand perspective of walking down the aisle of a plane and watching as people visibly recoil from the size of your body. Stacy used her craft to tell a story that too many fat travelers have experienced—a world where airline seats are too small and plus-size travelers are further humiliated by having to publicly ask for a seat-belt extender. It's just one example of how perpetuating the myth that certain people and certain needs are "abnormal" justifies our not doing anything about them. We shame people for looking or being a certain way, rather than shaming the industry for creating (or at least condoning) hostile environments for paying customers.

Letting these misconceptions proliferate is bad not just for the travelers experiencing discrimination but for our society as a whole. We miss out on learning about equity, inclusion, and acceptance—important lessons that in our increasingly polarized world we could stand to learn a little bit more about and put into better practice. These key values instead become replaced with something much darker: Discomfort. Bias. Fear. And that fear manifests itself in actions of discrimination and hate (France's ongoing headscarf and burkini ban, which has made its way in and out of the French Parliament since 2004, is a good example of how our myths and expectations of people, when unchallenged, can become major actions that affect millions). Fear is also one of the key drivers keeping many women away from traveling at all, which we'll talk about in the next chapter.

The good news is that things are being done about it. Communities like Plus Size Travel Too, created by Kirsty Leanne, and Fat Girls Traveling, created by Annette Richmond, offer body-positive trips and retreats that take into consideration the needs of plus-size people while centering the experience on respectful community and self-love. Stacy Bias's Flying While Fat Facebook group is a powerful space where users compare airplane seat measurements and offer helpful reviews of their experiences on different airlines.

The ability to create communities that give people safe spaces to ask questions and find common ground is one of the wonderful things that social media gave us. I can't tell you the number of times a user in our Wanderful Women Who Travel group on Facebook helped someone else along who needed it—offering a safe and comfortable place to sleep for someone whose flight was canceled, for example, or giving helpful travel tips to women visiting new places for the first time. So many amazing communities have helped break down barriers and connect people around the world, and a quick search can connect you with just about any type of group you can imagine.

These communities and groups help build just some of the pathways to being seen, but the other part of the equation is encouraging our society to build and innovate not just for the majority of us but for the people who are traditionally the most marginalized. "If you cater [to] and consider those at the margins of the margin, if you make sure that they are okay, then absolutely everybody else is taken care of," Jumoke explained brilliantly. "You cannot self-love your way out of bad policy."

As it stands, it's bad policies—and poor logistics—that limit us, more than our bodies ourselves. Let me say that again: Your body belongs in this world. If your body has trouble navigating this world, that's the system's fault, not yours.

This might sound like something you haven't heard before, but it's been a primary component of the Social Model of Disability since it was coined in the UK in the 1980s. The model suggests that it is our society and our environment that disable us, rather than our differences. Since body size is a protected class from discrimination in some places, I find that when we're combating systemic marginalization, the Social Model of Disability is a useful shared argument. As Elin Williams, creator of *My Blurred World*, a site that shares her experience living as a vision-impaired person, explained to me so well: "Society tells us our conditions are something that need fixing when, in reality, it's those attitudes and other barriers in society that need operating on."

When you are traveling with a disability, the thought experiment becomes even more powerful. Elin, for example, asked me to "imagine if all buildings, trains, and buses had step-free access; imagine if all travel information was provided in accessible formats like braille, audio, or easy read; imagine if people treated us as equal instead of like second-class citizens, we'd still be living with our impairments but we wouldn't be disabled because all the disabling barriers would have been removed. That's a world I'd love to live in, a world where I don't have to see."

For now, these limitations are palpable, and real. Elin relies on preplanning many of her trips in order to make her travels as seamless as possible. She is supremely organized, using packing cubes to divide her belongings and folders to access important documents easily. But while it certainly feels daunting sometimes, traveling for her is thrilling. "It can be so exhilarating," she said. "The sense of achievement I feel after completing an independent journey, even if it's purely just on the bus to my local town, is so unique and reminds me that I can do anything even if society tries to convince me I can't."

Marlene Valle, creator of the Deafinitely Wanderlust site and community for people who are Deaf or hard of hearing, can relate to the feeling of accomplishment in doing things on her own, as well as the nervousness and fear that come along with it—not just her own, but from her family and friends. She recalled the first time she told her family that she wanted to go on a solo trip. "My mind was ingrained by others' fears ('what if you didn't hear someone following behind you?') and how inaccessible the world is," she wrote to me. "I was both intrigued to see what our Mother Earth has to offer and real anxious about the thought of traveling into the unknown in our inaccessible world." While her family wanted what was best for her, the challenges of traveling alone as a Deaf person in a non-Deaf world seemed insurmountable for them. Missing a train stop because announcements were made over audio. Not having captioned videos or sign language services at popular attractions. Not having an alternative way to contact her hotel concierge besides calling.

While Marlene admits that traveling while Deaf isn't always easy, she has also found really exciting moments as a Deaf traveler. "There [is] beauty, and there are pains," she explained. "I find beauty in connecting with local hearing (non-Deaf) people through typing, writing, and gestures. There's beauty in bumping into local Deaf people, [when] we sometimes start off with 'Are you Deaf?' Although we have different cultures and sign language, we can sometimes still connect.

"No one community is a monolith," Marlene concluded.

"Because of my own privileges and challenges that impacted my travel experiences, I know that not every Deaf traveler will relate to me. I believe that storytelling is one of the powerful forms to make an impact and to create change—and I don't want to be the only one to do this. I want Deaf travelers to have a space to share their stories, especially where Deaf women can feel more connected to. I want to see all Deaf female travelers thrive—and know that it is, too, possible for them."

One key point that I've always appreciated about disability is the fact that you may become disabled at any point in your life. Just because you're not disabled now doesn't mean you won't be, or you won't have additional needs in the future. I still remember traveling with my friend Ned, who lived well into his adult life with two functioning legs and then lost them both from a staph infection. He was living in São Tomé at the time, but he actually got the infection at a dentist's office in Washington, DC, which was ironic given how many of his friends had worried about São Tomé's health-care system. I remember the long and arduous waits at the airport, the embarrassing moments when he had to endure being lifted by strangers, and watching him struggle to communicate his needs clearly in Portuguese. I was reminded of that experience when I had my first child, experiencing the long and winding pathways that we'd have to take our stroller on to find the single access ramp or elevator in an entire building or subway system (if it even existed).

If there's one thing that a lot of us can expect to experience, it's the process of aging (that is, if we're lucky enough). If you're reading this book and you're in your early twenties, it might feel like growing old is far off—but it approaches faster than you think. And when it comes to images and perceptions, the assumptions of a young, spry solo traveler couldn't be further from the truth. In 2018, market and consumer data provider Statista found that nearly 56 percent of leisure travelers in the UK were age fifty-five and older, with the largest bracket belonging to travelers over the age of seventy-five.[8] The US is not far behind, with the average solo traveler being about forty-seven years old, 84 percent of whom are women.[9]

You would think, knowing this, that the internet would be chock-full of images of mature, confident women travelers. I've lost count of the times I've talked to a new Wanderful member who joined after going through a recent divorce or the death of a partner, seeing solo travel as a way to explore a new aspect of her life that she hadn't tried before. In fact, the quantity of widowed and divorced women was so high at one point that we had a grief counselor hosting meetups in our Wanderful community that lasted strongly for nearly a year. Yet conventionally, the connection (or, let's be real, the lack thereof) between age and solo travel is simply not there. It's one of the reasons that content creators like Stacey Birch of the *Hot Flashes and Boarding Passes* blog and Charlotte Simpson of the *Traveling Black Widow* felt the motivation to start.

"I'd always been a travel gal and as my son aged and it gave me more independence, I would get back out there," Stacey recalled. "I'd look to Instagram for travel inspiration and I noticed while I was scrolling that no one looked like me! It was all young girls twirling in beautiful, dreamy locations."

With that she decided to launch her own Instagram account, filled with joy and loud, colorful images and statements—and her midlife self as the center focus. "There are so many preconceived ideas of aging and older women," Stacey shared, "so showing that we are fun and vivacious is super important." When Stacey pushes back on the narrative, it's not just about affirming her own abilities; her goal is to represent women everywhere. "It's applauded to get out and discover yourself and see the world when we're young. Spending money on solo travel as a woman is considered a midlife crisis thing, or 'trouble on the ol' home front.' Even when I am traveling alone at this age it's always met with disbelief. Hotel and restaurant staff will ask me if my husband is going out golfing."

Charlotte feels similarly: "My sister-in-law and I were in China, and there was an older woman by herself in our group celebrating her eightieth birthday. First-time solo travel at eighty! My sister and I were flabbergasted. That woman totally emboldened and empowered me, just her very presence! The next summer, I went to Italy, by myself. And I had a wonderful, wonderful time."

While Charlotte traveled a lot with her husband throughout their thirty-one-year marriage, she never expected to do it after he died. "When I traveled [while married] and would come across a solo woman I always thought, 'My gosh, she must not have any friends; what a horrible place to be that you've got to travel by yourself.'" Yet she found solo travels of her own to be an antidote to her grief. "It gives you such a huge thing to look forward to," she explained. "It activates your spirit a little bit."

When I asked her why she thinks people follow her so enthusiastically on Instagram, she laughed and said, "Well, I think that [what I'm sharing] is a little different from what they've seen from their own moms and grandmas." And it's true! Her images are bright, fun, and happy. Even in a single photo, you can see her joy from a mile away.

WHEN YOUR DIFFERENCES AREN'T AS VISIBLE

Of course, there are many qualities—what we believe, who we love, how our mind works, what we eat (or don't/can't eat)—that might not be immediately discernible in the way that size, race, ability, or age is. Sometimes you may choose to make certain identities visible, for example, by wearing a head covering, which may signal to someone that you're Muslim, Sikh, Hindu, or of another religious denomination. Other times you may choose not to, or not be able to.

My friend Jess Drucker, an LGBTQ+ relocation expert and the brilliant author of *How to Move Abroad (And Why It's the Best Thing You'll Do)*, told me stories about how her perception on "passing" (i.e., being perceived as straight) while traveling has changed over time. "When I was traveling before I had a family, I think passing was something I took for granted," she told me. "When I ran a travel blog, I was really resistant to being thought of as an LGBT travel blogger. I was like, 'Oh, what did I do today that was gay? I climbed the same volcano as you, I went to the same waterfall as you, I stayed in the same hostel as you.' But I did not understand at that time the complexities for many other people who weren't undergoing this thing of passing, because when you can't pass, or when someone does pick up on it, and you do come across hostility, then you did do something that was gay today, because just being you in an environment that may not be welcoming is a threat, and it is difficult."

Now Jess looks at passing differently. "Now that I'm a parent, and I have a family, I would never ever try to pass. I would never, ever let anyone misgender my spouse. When we are somewhere and someone says to my son, Theo, 'Go get your mommy,' I will say, 'I'm his mama. He also has a mommy.

Theo has two mommies.' Because every single thing in our environment must always signal to my kids that they should be proud of having two mommies."

I share this story because you may find you want to proudly make your differences visible. Maybe that's when you're in the safety of a group, or with a partner. There are travel groups that make it easy to travel without the challenges of preplanning for your needs—for example, Veg Jaunts and Journeys, founded by Kim Giovacco, and Green Earth Travel, founded by Donna Zeigfinger; both offer multiday tours specifically designed with vegans in mind. Olivia Travel, founded by Judy Dlugacz, hosts trips for LGBTQ+ women. You might not think of group travel and solo travel as even remotely related, but later in this book we'll talk about why they're practically sisters.

You may also find times when you don't feel comfortable or safe being open about your differences. That is a choice only you can make. However you identify, whatever needs you have, there are spaces for you. Even if what makes you different isn't obvious, or visible, or an identity I've highlighted so far in these pages, it doesn't mean that there aren't whole networks, entire ecosystems of people, who are in the same boat as you. As Zi Piggott, a Black non-binary entrepreneur and advocate who hails from Barbados, a place that only recently (in 2022) decriminalized gay sex, shared with me, "There's a safe space everywhere. Everywhere there will be a safe space." It's part of the reason that they* later founded Pink Coconuts, an international community of LGBTQ travelers.

---

* Zi prefers to use the pronouns "they/them" and "she/her" interchangeably, which you will see throughout this book.

While I believe firmly that everyone should go into a travel situation with a solid head on their shoulders and with a certain level of mental preparation, I also believe that sometimes the internet can leave us feeling more worried than when we started. It's the WebMD effect: You start searching for solutions to a small ailment and suddenly you believe you have three days to live and you haven't even consulted an actual medical professional yet. Researching travel tips on the internet isn't a dissimilar experience—because so many people are looking for information about the challenges of traveling, it seems the internet is disproportionately filled with search results full of fear and bad news. Trans and neurodivergent travel creator Kayley Whalen sees (and fights) that all the time, recognizing that most documentation about traveling while trans is related to safety.

"I want trans people to find joy," she told me. "You need to be aware of discrimination and sexism and transphobia, but don't let that prevent you from traveling. Go to a transgender cabaret in Thailand, hang out with GenderFunk or FTM Vietnam in Vietnam. Go to Spain, Portugal, Berlin, or Paris, the gayborhood in São Paulo, Brazil. There are these wonderful havens for trans people."

I spent time sitting down with a lot of community builders and creators to understand how their differences affect their travels and what they wish other travelers knew. Many of their stories made it into this chapter; but the point is not to give you a comprehensive list of people or to speak on behalf of everyone. I know I've left many stories untold, or imperfectly told. Still, I hope that this can be a start, a launchpad to show you that, no matter who you are, what identities you hold, or what accommodation you need, travel is possible for you. There is a community out there excited to welcome you.

I encourage you to follow these pioneers and others whose information you'll find in the Resources, beginning on page 269 to witness the work that is being done to make our world more accessible to everyone. The beauty of content creation and the growth of the creator industry over the last few years is that we have made spaces for so many new voices to share their realities on a public level with followers who can relate. I know that so far I haven't painted the prettiest picture for you of what social media has done to travel, but one truly incredible thing it has done for us is to expose us to opinions, beliefs, and lived experiences that are different from our own. In many ways, seeing those different perspectives, and seeing ourselves in those stories, makes travel feel achievable for all of us.

Whoever you are, whatever you look like, however you live, whomever you love—a travel mindset is available to you. *Travel* is available to you. You deserve to find yourself in places that you never imagined before. To challenge yourself with new experiences, to follow your curiosity, to step out of your comfort zone, and to accomplish things you never thought you were capable of. At some point someone may have told you otherwise—that your body, or your presence, is unusual, or abnormal, or ugly, or restricted. You may have even been led to believe it yourself. But you are valid. You are irreplaceable. You deserve space on this earth. You deserve to find your voice. No one will ever quite look or feel exactly the same as you. And like you, your travels are endlessly unique. They will never be the same for anyone else. And that, precisely, is the point.

Chapter 3

THE PERILS OF TRAVELING ALONE

"It is perfectly natural for the future woman to feel indignant at the limitations posed upon her by her sex. The real question is not why she should reject them: the problem is rather to understand why she accepts them."

—Simone de Beauvoir

AH, SAFETY. THE NUMBER ONE CONCERN OF EVERY WOMAN traveling solo (or so we're told), and probably at least one of the reasons you picked up this book—or it was given to you—in the first place.

To get us onto the same page (literally), I want to tell you a story. Curiously, though, it isn't a story about me. And it's not about you, either.

It's actually about my husband.

It was 2013, and my husband, Marvin, and I were meeting

up in Rio de Janeiro for a vacation. I'd been in the country for a few weeks for work and was a couple of hours behind him on a domestic flight. While I'm Portuguese American and fluent in Portuguese, Marvin had delicately practiced only three select phrases: "Onde é o banheiro?" (Where is the bathroom?); "Uma cerveja, por favor" (A beer, please); and "Não falo português" (I don't speak Portuguese). We'd figured that would be enough to get him through the couple of hours he'd be there without me.

He arrived at our destination, a friend's house in Santa Teresa, a beautiful neighborhood at the top of an enormous hill with a stunning view of Rio. He had very clear instructions on where to find the key and how to let himself in, but the key wasn't there. He would have called our friend, but, in true 2013 style, he'd skimped on getting a phone plan, deciding to rely solely on Wi-Fi to save money.

Now imagine you're in Marvin's position: You've just arrived in a new country where you don't speak the language, you're carrying an enormous suitcase, you're locked out of your accommodations, and your travel partner, who has a phone plan *and* a command of Portuguese, is still a few hours away.

If it were me, I'd freak out.

But not Marvin. No, Marvin approached a young couple walking down the street, pointed to his suitcase, and repeated "Americano! Americano!" loudly, over and over (I'm not exaggerating; this is exactly what he did). He was wearing a vacation hat. He had all of his belongings right on him—his credit cards, his passport. The couple stopped. They didn't speak English, but they invited him to come with them in Portuguese.

He followed, carrying his suitcase, down a narrow staircase, through some winding streets, and past numerous doorsteps darkened by curious observers. The houses got smaller and smaller, the doorsteps closer and closer to the street. A few minutes later he entered one of Rio's many *favelas*, or low-income settlements. The couple lived there.

They brought him inside their home and sat him down. They pulled out food and beer. They spent the next two hours passing messages back and forth on Google Translate. They became Facebook friends, listened to music together. The couple skipped their beach day to hang out with this intriguing stranger. Eventually, Marvin was able to contact our host and made his way back to our meeting point.

When I finally arrived in Rio, I had no idea of the adventures that Marvin had been on. He told me and a few of our Brazilian friends the story of his new amigos. Our eyes grew wide. "You visited a favela?" we asked, incredulous. I'd already considered Rio to be on the list of not-very-safe places; I couldn't imagine ever walking into a favela, let alone with no working phone, no language skills, and an enormous suitcase.

But he never thought anything of it.

If you're a woman reading this story, your reaction may likely have been the same as mine. As women, we are constantly told to be wary and watchful, especially when we're alone, and we're discouraged from spontaneity because our safety is the thing we've been programmed to think about every day of our lives. We are conditioned to rule out whole neighborhoods, and sometimes entire cities and even countries, and to search for lists of the safest places for women to travel as if they're instruction manuals (never mind the entirely problematic nature of ranking these places in the first place, as well as what it does to low-income communities, my own knee-jerk reaction to the favela notwithstanding).

And yet, it never even crossed my husband's mind to fear for his safety. Not even once.

Marvin's story is not uncommon among cis men. It's not unusual to hear a man talk about an amazing travel experience where he met some kind strangers, was taken under their wing, maybe even ended up getting an invitation to a party or spending a few days on their farm or going with them to a summer vacation spot.

Why don't as many women have these stories? We crave that same type of travel—connection, intimacy, shared experience, and adventure. In many ways, being able to have those moments is precisely what makes travel special. It's what differentiates a good trip from a truly great one, one that we remember forever. Yet the catch-22 is that those same meaningful travel experiences are the ones that require the level of trust we're being warned about. We don't have as many of these stories to tell because we've been told throughout our lives that those experiences are dangerous, especially for us. We are thrown between two narratives, constantly pushing and pulling their ways in and out of our psyches—one that inspires us to get out and see the world in rose-colored bliss and the other that scares the crap out of us (and our loved ones).

EAT, PRAY, LOVE OR *TAKEN*?

In case you're the one solo woman traveler who has not read *Eat, Pray, Love* yet (or watched the movie), let me distill this first narrative for you. Good-looking thirty-something Liz Gilbert (or Julia Roberts, in the movie) takes a 'round-the-world adventure to find herself after the disastrous end of her marriage. She indulges in fresh pasta and gelato. She finds deeper meaning in her life. She meets a gorgeous man who sweeps her off her feet in Bali. The world is filled with beauty.

This is the story we dream about—the story that gets us hoping and planning and visualizing the new versions of ourselves that we're going to find overseas. The picture-perfect shot of us gazing wistfully at a beautiful vista or with our hands outstretched to the sky in gratitude.

But almost like a disappointing "gotcha" moment, while I'm dreaming about my own Italian villa in the countryside and my quirky but cute neighbors, and my evenings spent stomping my own grapes in the dusty old winery I'll discover with the irresistible hottie down the street (sorry, Marvin!), there's this other narrative that the media is serving me at the same time. And even if I'm not keeping tabs on this other narrative, my parents certainly are, because that narrative sounds an awful lot like the movie *Taken*, where Liam Neeson's daughter is kidnapped by Albanian human traffickers while on vacation in France, and he fully dedicates his (sexy Irish crime-fighting) life to saving her.

So either we're rapaciously indulging in food and wine and la dolce vita or we're being kidnapped and killed overseas. There's no in-between. These two stories, ever so different, are served to us side by side, over and over in a vicious cycle of novels and news stories. We think of solo travel for women as either absolutely delightful or prohibitively dangerous. It's never somewhere in the middle.

Perhaps it's not surprising, then, that so many of us have canceled trips, rerouted flights, and stopped travel dreaming because we were—or someone told us we should be—afraid of going out into the world by ourselves. So we put off our travels until we can find someone to go with us. Or we stop traveling altogether. In fact, a Wanderful survey found that nearly 40 percent of women have opted out of a trip because we were concerned about our safety or because of a family member who was concerned about our safety.[1]

See the issue here? Not traveling—not letting ourselves be visible in the world—makes us invisible again. It further perpetuates the myth that women can't or won't travel, or that the world isn't safe enough for us. If something bad happens, the belief is that we're exclusively responsible for those outcomes, and it seems the only way to be safe is to just stay home. That myth doesn't affect just us. It changes the way our larger society perceives us, too.

Here's another story: It's 2013 and I'm at a Starbucks in Chicago, scrolling the news on my laptop, a caramel latte in hand. A headline hits me. It's a story in the *New York Times* about thirty-three-year-old Sarai Sierra, a Staten Island mom of two killed while solo traveling in Türkiye.[2]

The article is scary and dark. It's filled with gossip and mystery. Was she cheating on her husband and embroiled in a love affair with a Turk? Was she dealing drugs in Amsterdam? Why was she walking on this or that street, staying in this or that place? Why did she seem so unafraid to travel by herself? What exactly happened?

We attempt to feel better by telling ourselves that there is a reason behind what happens to women like Sarai Sierra. Perhaps she did something wrong or went somewhere she wasn't supposed to. Perhaps she was too bold, not cautious enough.

The world is a dangerous place for women—she should have known better.

Her death was horrifying and tragic, but it was the comments section that really shocked me.

Hundreds of readers from around the world shared their thoughts, and instead of expressing sadness or pity for this poor woman, they said things like:

What kind of mother would leave her two children and travel to Istanbul by herself?

What kind of husband would let his wife travel alone?

And yes, even *She should have known better.*

My stomach churned.

Of course *she got killed abroad*, the comments seemed to imply. *She was doing something she wasn't supposed to. She was selfish. She was a bad mom. She deserved it.*

Right?

But then again, what kind of world have we created where moms who travel alone—where caregivers who take time to nurture themselves—are selfish?

Why are we assuming that the victim did something wrong and that she's fully responsible for her demise? Is it possible that she was just in the wrong place at the wrong time? Why do we so firmly insist that every time something bad happens it was fully preventable and the result of the victim's poor judgment?

The fact is that women around the world are victims of violence every day, both domestically and abroad. What was it about this story that garnered so many clicks? What embedded biases do we have about white women who are killed in predominantly brown and Black communities that make stories like this irresistible clickbait (stories that have been republished in various forms by various media for years and years)? What types of biases are we further cementing by continuing to spotlight these stories while selectively ignoring others?

FEAR HELPS US AND HURTS US

For thousands of years, fear and safety have gone hand in hand. It's fear that has protected us and helped us avoid danger. We are hardwired as humans to spread bad news faster than good news, because in history spreading bad news quickly has saved our lives. The problem comes when that fear is misguided. When bad news morphs into an enormous game of "telephone," with each person who retells the news leaving out or playing up a critical detail, changing the intention of the original message entirely. Rather than becoming a source of helpful information, it transforms into overgeneralizations and quick fixes. Maybe those are physical products, like pepper spray hidden in fake lipstick containers, or nail polish that changes color in the presence of a date rape drug. Maybe it becomes fast media, like clickbait lists of the "safest" countries for women to travel alone (as if you could rank an entire country). But these solutions have one thing in common: They put the responsibility on our shoulders as women to protect ourselves, and further cement the belief that if something goes wrong, it is our own fault.

"There are so many articles that say, 'Hey woman traveler, here's how you can stay safe and avoid being attacked,'" said Jumoke of the Triple Cripples. "But they're having this conversation with the wrong people, because the people being spoken to are not the ones who are doing these things. Even the framing of these questions is completely inappropriate. We shouldn't be talking about how to keep this from happening to you. I don't want it happening to anyone."

Our culture of victim-blaming in interpersonal violence is alive and well, and it shows its teeth when women experience violence abroad. No one understands that better than Paula Lucas, the founder of Pathways to Safety, an organization that was created to support victims of gender-based violence abroad. "If someone is sexually assaulted, we ask, 'Well, why were you wearing that? Why were you out? Why did you drink?' All the blame goes on the victim," Paula said. "We never tell people who were robbed, 'Why were you wearing that fancy suit? Why did you have such a nice house?' In interpersonal violence, the victim is blamed. It is always the responsibility of the traveler to stay safe and it doesn't seem fair."

When something bad does happen to someone, it's those stories that are being told, because they're juicier and more exciting (from a media perspective, anyway) than the ones about everything going fine and well. And when these horrors happen to white women, they take on a new level of collective anguish, and they make headlines faster. Digging up tantalizing details about possible unfaithfulness leading to a murder in a mysterious place is not only gossip-worthy; it helps justify what happened, as if this problem started with the traveler and not with our society as a whole.

The solution, then, to making the world a safer and better place for women isn't to stop traveling and stay home. Nor is it to stock up on promising safety products and wag a finger at everyone else. The solution is to do our part to combat these negative stereotypes. To show how many different types of people actually *are* traveling. To push back on the narrative that travel is perfect or, conversely, too dangerous to try. And to advocate for more inclusive, thoughtful, and equitable spaces where all of us can not just coexist but thrive.

WHAT SAFETY REALLY MEANS

If you've gotten this far in the chapter and your takeaway is, "Wow, Beth says that fears about solo travel are overblown and, realistically, nothing bad will happen, and that anyone who suggests otherwise is feeding into clickbait," then you're reading it wrong. At the end of the day, solo travel for women has become a bit of a self-fulfilling prophecy: The more we tell women that traveling alone is unsafe for them, and the more we as an international society continue to perpetuate that norm, the more it really *does* feel unsafe to be, or to travel, alone.

While we can't solve the state of the universe, there are some guiding principles that can help you approach questions of your own safety in a more nuanced, thoughtful way:

1. **Your definition of safety is relative and personal.** Safety means different things to different people, depending on the intersection of their identity and where they're traveling.
2. **Nowhere in the world is 100 percent safe.** Sadly, bad things happen in "safe" places. Wonderful things happen in "dangerous" places. Before you cross an entire country off your list, make sure you're taking the time to understand the nuances of the place you're visiting.
3. **No matter how much you may prepare, many of these issues are systemic.** Sexism, racism, ableism, economic disparity—many of the drivers of violence and crime

against women are not things that can necessarily be solved with pepper spray, but taking those systems into account can give us footing to find our own confidence and to take certain narratives with a grain of salt.

YOUR DEFINITION OF SAFETY IS RELATIVE AND PERSONAL

On a trip with her mom to Amsterdam, Justine Abigail Yu heard a familiar refrain: "Massage lay-dee, massage lay-dee!" a man yelled at her from a side street. His insinuation was that she was a masseuse or sex worker. She was neither.

"As a Filipina Canadian and as an Asian woman, I have felt and still continue to feel the weight of exoticization and fetishization," Justine, the founder of Living Hyphen, a community and magazine that explores the experiences of hyphenated Canadians, explained. "As an Asian woman, I am expected to be a modest, quiet, submissive, and subservient object—all the things that I am not. And I should note that this is not unique to travel but a very real stereotype that I experience on a regular basis both at home and abroad. The precarity of my safety is only heightened when I'm traveling because I may not know the local language, the emergency lines to call, or my way around the city."

These are issues Justine faces all the time at home, but when she's abroad she has to consider them under different circumstances. "Traveling around Asia as an Asian woman is actually where I am hypervigilant of my identity," Justine says. "When I find myself traveling around Southeast Asia in heavily expat-populated or visited areas, I am always on high alert assessing the white male gaze that follows me (and all other Asian women around me) so heavily and intensely."

This experience isn't just limited to Justine's identity as a Filipina Canadian. Martinique (Marty) Lewis, creator of the ABC Travel Green Book, founder of the Black Travel Alliance, and host of National Geographic's *Black Travel Across America*, shared a similar story. "For me, I'm even more on the lookout traveling through America than I am traveling internationally," she explained. "In general, my head is always on a swivel. When I go to Europe, I do understand that in places that are remote, where there aren't a lot of Black people, they will think I'm a prostitute. I'm used to that now." Marty recalled an experience in Latvia when she went out to dinner with friends and a group of men stood at the window openly staring at them. "For us, it's always being fetishized, people thinking that you're this thing that they want. And they call you every single name of the book: Beyoncé, Alicia Keys, Tyra Banks."

These experiences remind us that safety is often a matter of context. As comforting as it may be to imagine that there's a one-size-fits-all rubric to keep you safe from physical, mental, or sexual harm, your personal safety actually is extremely relative. Some of that is specific to the place you're visiting, like the crime rate. But other elements are much more nuanced and have to do with your identity and your social location, your level of travel experience, your risk tolerance (i.e., how uncomfortable you're willing to get), and other qualities that make up what I like to call your personal risk profile.

UNDERSTANDING YOUR PERSONAL RISK PROFILE

There's a reason for the adage "There's safety in numbers," and I can't pretend there aren't certain elements of a trip that do make you more vulnerable as a solo woman traveler and are pretty much unavoidable. By and large, traveling on your own makes you more of a target than traveling with a group. You're more exposed. You don't have the luxury of another person's eyes and ears looking out for you. You don't have the physical security of a group of bodies. And you probably don't have a knowing and competent guide like many group travelers have.

It is also true that different countries have different expectations and customs around gender norms. When you travel to a place, you often operate under *the host country's* norms and customs, not your own (with some select exceptions, which we'll discuss in chapter 5, where visitors are held to a different standard than local women).

But just as everyone travels with a different travel muscle, so does everyone travel with a different personal risk profile—that is, a set of truths that may include:

- Your racial or ethnic background, your sexual orientation, your religion, or your gender identity. (How accepting of me will this community be, and how will that affect my experience there? What is the history of this place in general and with people who look like me?)
- Your physical body. (How accessible is this place to me and how will I feel traveling there with my body and my mobility constraints, if any?)
- Your language. (How well can I understand and communicate with others around me?)
- Your lived experience. (Am I dealing with past trauma or experiences that have created certain expectations around my future travels? Have I traveled alone before?)
- Your neurodiversity. (How do I interpret the world around

me, and to what degree am I prepared to handle the unfamiliar?)

- Your connections. (Are there local communities that I can tap into for support in this place?)

Your personal risk profile isn't an exact science. You won't get a "score" at the end of it. Instead, it's a series of questions that I want you to think about as you approach each solo adventure. Taking time to evaluate the elements above will help set the foundation for understanding the level of threat to your personal safety you may encounter, which you can weigh against your risk tolerance.

The value of seeing personal safety as a set of contexts you'll encounter, rather than a checklist of protocols, is that it allows you to observe how your risk level changes with location and time. Your personal risk profile isn't just a onetime self-evaluation, because it's always changing. How safe or unsafe you feel about a location—how accessible it is, how accepting people are, how different you may appear—changes based on your experience level and where you go. Even the "where" is nuanced—you might experience the same city three different times, with the only difference being the neighborhood you visited, the time of year you went, or the fact that you felt more comfortable because you'd already been there twice before.

Your definition of safety may look different to you depending on who you are or what you look like, as well as what your physical, mental, and emotional needs are at a given moment. Your social location—or, rather, how the intersections of your identity interact with your geographic location and that local culture—will change based on the place you're in. For Justine, traveling to Asia as an Asian woman affects her in a different way than traveling in Canada and North America; it's also different depending on how touristy the area she's visiting is.

When you travel, that social location may shift rather quickly. It reframes how others perceive you, but it also may reframe how you think about yourself. You might "blend in" more in one place and stick out somewhere else. You might feel more at ease in one location and more alert in another, simply because of the social dynamics of this new place.

Try taking an international plane ride from a cold place to a warm place and you'll see a physical manifestation of all of this. You get on a plane in cold Boston and everyone is covered head to toe in long winter coats with that quintessential grumpy New England winter face. Then you arrive in Port-au-Prince and suddenly it's like everyone has peeled a layer of skin off—the coats have miraculously disappeared and people are dressed in warm-weather attire and everyone is speaking Haitian Kreyòl. When you first board the plane, the pilot says, "Welcome aboard," and when you leave, they're saying, "Mèsi paske w te chwazi American Airlines." It's like this new location has totally changed everyone.

But the changes might be internal, as well. You might perceive yourself to be more relaxed and open (or, conversely, more tense and closed off), and that in itself will change you and, in effect, change how others see you, too. It's a constantly renewing cycle of perception, interpretation, and reality. When Jumoke talked with me about safety, she shared how she knows that "being a woman but also being disabled and also being Black, my welcome to a space might be different to your welcome to space." No identity is inherently "safe" or "unsafe"—it always depends on your context.

NOWHERE IN THE WORLD IS 100 PERCENT SAFE

Okay, Beth, you might be thinking, *I hear you that context is critical, but aren't some places just, you know, unsafe?* Well, that's a good question. Let's say you're trying to figure out if a destination is safe or not. What's the right way to begin? If you're like me, you might try to look at some hard data (as they say, numbers never lie, right?). You pull up a report on the number of violent acts per capita committed in the place you're visiting. But what if I were to tell you that even this information can be interpreted incorrectly and should be analyzed with care?

Let's take Chicago, for example, long known as one of the most violent cities in America with the country's highest murder rate. When I lived in Chicago, I would regularly get calls from concerned family and friends who heard violent news stories on TV. And, truth be told, there was a guy who got shot in the butt on our block. But a 2022 article in *Crain's Chicago Business*[3] might give you a different story if you take a moment to break the data down further.

We've established that Chicago has the United States' highest number of murders. But have you taken population into account? Factoring in the size of America's fourth-largest city, Chicago's per capita murder rate becomes lower than that of neighboring cities like Detroit, Milwaukee, and St. Louis.[4]

What about neighborhood? In Chicago, your specific location in the city makes an enormous difference. Garfield Park, located on Chicago's West Side, has a higher murder rate than the world's "most dangerous" city, Tijuana, Mexico (at 146.8

murders per 100,000 residents, according to data from the University of Chicago Crime Lab). But Lincoln Square, located just seven miles north, has a per capita murder rate of 3.4, about the same as Virginia Beach or Zurich.[5] Data can be wildly different based on neighborhood or even block.

In the scheme of things, Chicago is a pretty specific example. But understanding the nuances of a city like Chicago should help you understand that no city is completely unsafe, and furthermore, no *country* is completely unsafe, either.

I know the internet will try to convince you otherwise. It'll try to whet your travel appetite with a list of the twenty-three best countries for solo female travelers or the ten safest destinations around the world. You will be so, so tempted to read them, if for no other reason than because you're just really curious. But these lists are complete and utter hogwash. Here's why:

- **You can't rank an entire country.** I mean, have you *been* to a country before? (You clearly have because you likely live in one.) The United States is a classic example. I remember a conversation with a good friend from Portugal who was planning a visit to the States. She was terrified, absolutely *terrified*, about going to work at a summer camp in rural Vermont. "I know people are shot in the streets in America," she said to me. "Should I be afraid?" If you're an American reading this, you're probably chuckling right now. *Vermont? You're more likely to get hurt hitting a moose with your car.* This question was asked of me fifteen years ago, but nowadays, the question feels less innocent. Our statistics of mass killings and hate crimes have put America on many countries' warning lists recently. But this is exactly what I mean when I say entire countries are completely unrankable. There are places in every country that are dangerous; there are also comparatively safer places in every country (and as we established earlier, how dangerous it is for *you* depends often and unfortunately on who you are). The degree of safety also changes with time, not just over years or generations but over months with variables like political climate, war, disease, and natural disaster.

- **These lists can become breeding grounds for prejudices about race and income.** I have seen lists that have attempted to rank places as safe or unsafe based on community surveys of how people "felt" when walking around different places. But our "feelings" are often rooted in dangerous biases of our own, and often those biases are centered on race and income. My sense that I'm unsafe in a particular neighborhood may have more to do with my own internally embedded racism and classism than any actual facts about crime in the area. They also, as we know, leave out important nuances about social location. Driving around after dark in the southern United States by myself may feel fine for a white woman, but what about for a woman of color? Traveling to the UK and Australia might appear to be safer because they're English-speaking destinations, but does that change for a traveler who doesn't speak English? These lists often target the broadest swath of imaginary readers possible, further perpetuating the myth that the "travelers" out there are young, white, Western adventurers—and that all our needs are the same, when they're not.
- **Lists like these focus on trends of violence rather than other important criteria like systemic racism or sexism.**

The lists that try to take the most scientific approach by comparing data points about violence—like the example we just reviewed in Chicago—may seem the most reliable, but what is a reliable measurement of safety, anyway? Maybe acts of violence per capita is one, but what exactly were those acts of violence? There have been cities in America that experienced a church massacre or school shootings, driving up their statistics, but that otherwise have impeccable crime rates. There are other places in our country that have high crime rates because of mostly highly targeted acts of gang violence that don't often happen in touristy areas (though to be fair, concerns about violence to innocent bystanders are absolutely valid and real). If we look at data about incarcerations, are we prepared to deeply understand the massive problems with our justice system and the fact that nearly half of all incarcerated people are convicted for drug-related crimes (and that this data is less a reflection of the safety of an area and more a reflection of how much overhaul our justice system needs)?

These lists do more than just misrepresent many places around the world. They also deeply affect tourism, which for many places can economically make or break them. Places that are constantly recommended, over and over again, by listicles like these run the risk of severe over-tourism, which can crush environments and dampen residents' quality of life. But other places left off this list—or, worse, listed as places *not* to visit (yes, those lists exist, too)—can suffer debilitating losses of tourism that are difficult to recover from. The results fuel a vicious cycle—without a significant financial investment (and sometimes even *with* lots of money being thrown at the problem), it can be difficult for a place to rebrand itself as a great travel destination when it's been labeled otherwise, and that missed income makes it difficult to invest in the very things that appeal to travelers, like new construction, updated infrastructure, and even sleek marketing campaigns.

It turns out that this mythical norm concept continues to bite us—by imagining that travel is enjoyed by only a small minority, we create generalizations about safety and nonspecific advice that end up hurting whole other communities because of our own ingrained biases. When someone tells you to go (or not to go) somewhere, you should think about what may have shaped their worldview before taking their advice.

MANY OF THESE ISSUES ARE SYSTEMIC

This may not make you feel better, but at the end of the day many of the qualities that indicate to us that a place is unsafe for us—sexism, racism, ableism, economic disparity—come from much larger systems that we won't solve with one product, listicle, or TED talk. But knowing that they're there, and understanding our part in their presence, can give us proper footing moving forward. Because yes, even we travelers play a part.

We must recognize that tourism—the industry that supports travel—is often very highly curated. It is interpreted through tour guides, tourism boards, marketing campaigns, and more. Marty Lewis understands this on a profound level, constantly pushing back on others' recommendations to travel to (or avoid) certain areas. She tells one particularly enlightening story about visiting Costa Rica and asking her tourism partners to visit the Limón Province, which has strong Afro-Caribbean roots.

"They tell people [to not] even get off the boat when the cruise ship stops [in Limón]," she lamented. "They tell people there's nothing to do, [but] then there's all this history. And they tell people to stay away. People don't understand that this is systematically set up this way, so that business is not driven into those BIPOC communities. They tell people do not go to Limón. But what is the reason? Oh, because there's crime there. Well, that's interesting, because there's crime in San José, too, and you send more people there. There's more crime in San José than there was in Limón. And not only that, but the crime was there because you put it there. You push the people out of San José and sent them there. So not only did you facilitate this crime, you're making sure that no tourism comes there even though cruise ships stop there."

Understanding the "why"—as well as the "why not"—is essential to uncovering real stories in travel. When we are encouraged to travel to a place, why are we encouraged to travel there rather than somewhere else? When we experience inequities, what larger systems have contributed to this moment? How can we push back on these narratives, and what is our personal risk limit in doing that? These questions aren't easy. They're complicated. That's exactly why we should ask them.

FAMILIAR IS NOT ALWAYS SAFER

I want to take a moment to go back to this earlier point about a place "feeling" safer than another place. If you ever find yourself "feeling" a certain way about a place, I want you to take a moment to think about where that feeling comes from.

Oftentimes, we as humans confuse the feeling of familiarity with the feeling of safety. Evolutionarily, this has served us. The things we were familiar with were likely to be safer than the things we were not, because we had clearly survived exposure to those things at one point or another, which was why we crossed paths with them again.

But the downside is that sometimes the familiar ties us down. It makes us more hesitant to try new foods, for example (I'll admit, I am a perfect case here, preferring to cozy up to a bowl of pad thai or yellow curry at our local Thai restaurant rather than order something new and run the risk of—gasp!— *not liking it*). But the effects are darker, too. They also at least partially contribute to the reason we may put up with an abusive partner, or a job we hate—because the fear of the unknown is greater than the familiar.

This confusion between familiarity and safety strikes us in a travel context as well. We might worry about the safety of an upcoming destination, not realizing that our own home may very well be statistically more dangerous. Because a destination is unfamiliar, we get mixed up.

There is some element of truth, of course, to the concerns about traveling away from home: In a foreign place you may not be aware of local customs, rules, and regulations. You could be more likely to be caught off guard or unaware while you're busy navigating unfamiliar streets and taking in new sites on your own.

But you also run the risk of being much more complacent in a place you call home, especially if you're deeply rooted in the expectation that you're safe there.

SOMETIMES FEELING IS ALL WE HAVE

While I may seem to be putting a lot of negative energy out toward the concept of feeling a certain way, at the end of the day, sometimes a feeling is all we have. I want you to hold two conflicting truths in the same space, because the reality is that they're both extremely important.

The first truth is that when we're traveling alone, sometimes we simply won't know the right (or "safest") thing to do and will need to listen to our gut.

The other truth is that sometimes our gut is prejudiced.

Yup, I said it. We are all imperfect humans. You might be walking down the street in an unknown place with that "feeling" at the pit of your stomach that something's wrong. And maybe you're right—maybe that gut feeling will ultimately get you out of a tight predicament and back into the welcoming arms of safety and you'll be thanking your lucky stars later. But it's also possible that your gut has been affected by an entire lifetime of systemic racism and classism and generalizations about places that you should and shouldn't visit and people that you should and shouldn't interact with. Maybe that's why I would have recoiled from the prospect of visiting a favela but my husband didn't think otherwise. And if that's the case, that "gut feeling" you're having is actually an example of you operating within this system. The tricky part is, you're going to have to decide which scenario is which.

You're going to have moments when you're faced with the predicament of uncomfortably going with the flow, either because women have been socialized to do so for centuries, because you're just not feeling brave enough to speak up, or because you're going against your gut on purpose, and then you're only going to find out later if that tightening in your stomach was valid or not.

You're also going to have moments in your travels where you're truly questioning that gut feeling because you're surrounded by unfamiliar territory. Is that guy whistling at me dangerous, or just part of a moderately chauvinistic society? Is this person getting too close to me, or is that just how people stand in this country? Just as you may have trouble interpreting others' intentions and nonverbal cues, others may have trouble interpreting yours. We don't have a lifetime of cultural context to inform us, so we have to make the best decisions we can for ourselves. At the end of the day, your life is your life.

The goal here, of course, is not to force you to endure situations that feel unsafe and gaslight you into believing they're fine. If you feel unsafe, trusting your intuition is the absolute best thing that you can do. You may never know why. But when you can, it may help to ask yourself this question: *Am I feeling this discomfort because of a bias, or is there an actual safety concern here?*

Of course, there are hundreds of ways to practice safety precautions to limit your risk when traveling in the first place: When leaving your hotel, tell your concierge that you're stepping out. Have your address written down on a piece of paper in the local language. Don't take out a map or your cell phone while walking down the street. Know your area and don't walk alone in dark places at night. You can learn more tips in any number of blog posts and e-books about solo travel.

Safety Starts Before Your Trip

We might not be able to always stop bad things from happening, but there are a few quick and easy ways you can look out for that "future self" if you do experience something and need help:

- Write down important numbers in advance, especially an emergency contact that you may want to call if something happens to you. You might have a hard time bringing this number to mind later.
- Make a copy of your passport and keep it in a safe place in case the real copy is stolen. You might also consider digitally saving a picture in a safe, password-protected place (read: *not* your phone!) so that you can access it in case of emergency.
- Write down the local emergency number in your destination and make sure your phone has an international data plan or an eSIM (which functions like a digital version of a SIM card). Most countries can make emergency calls without a SIM card, but not all.
- Do your research on the culture of the place you're visiting, and talk to other women who are from there.
- Make sure you've notified the embassy nearest your destination of your travels so they can contact you in case of emergency. (In the US use the State Department's Smart Traveler Enrollment Program, or STEP.)

One may call these tips common sense, but if you don't practice them and something does happen to you, perpetuating the myth that *you* were at fault because you didn't adequately prepare yourself is wrong. It creates a culture of victim-blaming that none of us needs right now. It's also what creates articles and comments that perpetuate a fear of the *perils* of solo female travel. That's wrong, too.

No one's solo travel experience will be quite the same as anyone else's. It's not just because the activities you pick and the places you stay will be different from everyone else's. It's because *you* are different from everyone else. Your life history and your lived experiences, your personal risk profile, your unique social location, your choice to visit a particular place at a particular moment in time, that place's current political and social environment, its embedded history, plus your own set of expectations and judgments, all weave themselves together to create a complicated web of factors that make this concept of "safety" nearly impossible to distill in a top 10 list. Your job is not to master these factors. It is to give space to these truths and these realities at once. Not to avoid the unknown at all costs, but to feel confident and to trust your ability to handle the unexpected. Not to stop fear from happening in the first place—but to acknowledge that fear and to proceed boldly into the unknown anyway.

A Few More Basic Safety Tips

Only you can decide what lets you feel safe, but any solo traveler should consider the following when they hit the road on their own:

1. Get to know your surroundings. Take a walk in the daytime and make note of certain landmarks that you can point out later if you're lost.
2. Write down the name and address of your hotel in the local language. Include a pronunciation guide if you need

it. If you're staying at an Airbnb, include cross streets or a nearby restaurant, so you don't have to give a taxi driver or a stranger on the street your exact address.

3. Be conscious of where you pull out your phone or map on the street. If possible, duck into a shop or a restaurant first. Making it obvious that you don't know where you're going can make you a mark, and the distraction of a map can be a boon to would-be pickpockets.

4. Don't take a taxi off the street. Instead, ask a restaurant or hotel employee to call one for you, so you can be sure it's a reputable service. Or use a ridesharing service you know so your location is on record and if you have any issues (with your service or otherwise), you will know who to call.

5. Be aware. Keep your money close to you, leave valuables at home, and keep your eyes open. A guy once told me to carry a roll of quarters in my fist so I could punch people harder. Please don't do that.

And the big one: Should you pretend to not be alone? Ultimately, the answer is up to you. You may feel more comfortable pretending your friend or significant other is just around the corner, or keeping the TV running in your hotel room so it looks like someone's there. Ultimately, the decision is more about how much you want to keep up the act. In the past, I've found it too exhausting, but you may feel otherwise. That's up to you.

Part Two

EMBRACING THAT TRAVEL MINDSET

Chapter 4

SOLO DOESN'T HAVE TO MEAN SINGLE

"She remembered who she was and the game changed."
—Lalah Delia

WHEN I FIRST STARTED TRAVELING ALONE, I HATED THAT moment when I checked into a hotel by myself. The hotel receptionist would greet me with a warm welcome. They'd reach for my driver's license or my passport. And then at the end, they'd always ask the dreaded question: "How many keys do you want?"

There wasn't anything wrong with the question, of course. But usually, it was my first time hearing someone else—or, perhaps, hearing myself explain to someone else—that I was on my own. Up to that point, I could have been in any situation. Maybe at the airport I was grabbing a snack while my husband picked up a magazine from the Hudson News shop. Maybe I was taking the bus to a girls' getaway or a family reunion. But upon check-in at my hotel, it was one of the first times I had to declare out loud to another person that I was solo.

"Just one," I would say to the receptionist in Los Angeles, or Tel Aviv, or Auckland. But every time I responded that way, I knew I was betraying myself. That word "just" was filled with so much meaning. Like I was *supposed* to be with someone else, but it didn't work out. It felt like the self-infliction of the "Where's your boyfriend?" question that, I'm sorry to say, many solo women still get when traveling on our own (sometimes as a well-meaning inquiry, other times as a pickup line, and always with a sexist—not to mention heteronormative—undertone, however benign).

I was my own worst enemy—confirming that I was the exception to the rule, an unusual creature out of its natural habitat.

Finding comfort in my solo travels first started with directly confronting my own self and the expectations I had, which in many ways mirrored the expectations that our society places on us. Usually those consist of a few things, including:

- That you have to be single to travel solo.
- That solo travel happens *to* you (often because of a cancellation or change of plans), rather than being a choice you actively make.
- That not only are you single but you're *ready to mingle* (whether that means meeting new friends, or flirting, dating, and hooking up).
- That if you're not automatically ready to mingle, be prepared because you are going to be ridiculously lonely and awkward the whole time.

All of these assumptions coexist in a universe that tells women we shouldn't be alone (ever), that there's no reason why we would want to be alone, and that if we do find ourselves alone, we're going to be bored and miserable. This perception is so widespread that we think and believe it ourselves, and even if we manage to overcome it and take ourselves on a solo trip, we still say things like "just one." *Just.* Like we're apologizing for our existence in the world.

Talk to anyone who has been traveling solo for years, however, and you're going to hear an entirely different story. That's because we believe we know one of the world's best-kept secrets: We don't travel alone because we have to. We travel alone because it nourishes us.

Solo travel helps us to reconnect with ourselves in a way we couldn't otherwise. It takes us out of familiar contexts and allows us to make our own choices and follow our own desires. It gives us a chance to experience the world the way *we* want to, and not through the lens of another person. And it allows us to engage with others in a way that we wouldn't be able to otherwise when shielded by the protective cover of a travel buddy or a group.

I know for a fact that you don't hear that side of the story enough. The side of the story where women *choose* to travel alone, and do so happily, for a wide variety of reasons. This side of the story doesn't usually make it into a fearmongering news report or a Top 10 Safest Places list. So we're going to talk about it here.

In this chapter, we'll take a look at what solo travel actually means and some of the incredible things that come out of solo trips. We'll rethink the meaning and the purpose of traveling alone, and I'll even give you a few travel activities and tactics to ponder that you might not have ever considered would fit into the solo travel definition to begin with. I'll prescribe some easy steps, and some more challenging ones, to help you start shifting your paradigm about what a solo trip is and what you should get from it. And I'll try to make a few jokes along the way (if you're lucky, you might even find them funny).

ALONE DOESN'T ALWAYS MEAN LONELY

Let's kick this off with one of our biggest pieces of solo travel fake news there is: that it's lonely. And that you'll be lonely when you do it. It's like a bad eHarmony commercial: You, playing tennis by yourself, running back and forth across the court. You, laughing over a cocktail and a pupu platter for two, solo. You, getting a couple's massage, the other bed empty.

It is true that traveling with another person can be a ton of fun. But it doesn't mean that when you travel by yourself you're just one half of a person or that you should expect any less of an adventure. In fact, you may find that traveling alone gives you more access to people you never would have met before (if you choose, of course).

Let's take a minute to redefine exactly what solo travel means. Solo travel means that you are taking your own adventure in the way you want. It means that you're not tied to another person's agenda. It means that you're free to make your own choices, whether in the planning of your trip or while on the trip itself. It means *you* get to decide what to do with your time and where to spend it. Solo travel is a chance for you to connect with yourself and your own needs. And as long as you are focusing on your needs and making your own plans, there are numerous ways that a solo trip can manifest.

You also don't need to start cold turkey. Your first solo trip doesn't have to happen in complete isolation or for a long period of time. Revising what types of travel are solo trips plays a key part in giving yourself permission to bite off smaller chunks of solo travel rather than diving into the deep end. The great thing about traveling alone is that you get to decide precisely what you want to do, and that includes how much interaction with other people you have. If you're not particularly interested in being by yourself, you can stay at a hostel and surround yourself with other travelers. You can sign up for a class, join a Meetup, or use VolunteerMatch to find a volunteer opportunity. You can take a food or walking tour.

Organizations like VAWAA (which lets you apprentice with a local artist); Workaway (where you get room and board in exchange for work); or WWOOF (where you can work on an organic farm) offer really neat ways to travel solo while also learning from another person at the same time. Sojrn and Remote Year are programs that offer the logistical support many solo travelers crave while also giving you the freedom and flexibility to determine your own schedule, while keeping your day job. I once knew a woman who signed up for a one-week photography class in Nicaragua. What a cool way to give yourself some structure, without compromising your autonomy.

TAP INTO THE POWER OF COMMUNITY

Did you know there are entire communities full of people dedicated to helping one another when they travel and combating loneliness before it even starts? That was the founding principle of companies like Couchsurfing and Airbnb, the former of which still hosts meetups that anyone can attend to meet other travelers (you can even attend them in your home city). It's the whole purpose of Wanderful, a space where traveling women have a live support network and a local contact on the ground wherever they go. We now have more than fifty local hubs worldwide that you can tap into, as well as plenty of travel-loving women outside of our hubs who will meet up with you for a cup of coffee or host you in their home (and, yes, this is a shameless pitch for my own company, but I promise we're pretty great).

Plugging into local networks like these can help take the edge off those initial "Oh my goodness, am I going to actually do this?" jitters. Startups like Eatwith and Traveling Spoon have created the "Airbnb for dinner" economy, bringing together groups of strangers to share a home-cooked meal in someone's house. Hostels often host group excursions and walking tours. Platforms like TrustedHousesitters allow you to house-sit for someone and take care of their pets while they're away, giving you instant access to a home and a four-legged companion. Communities and activities like this can help you find your footing while you're still battling the "table for one" demons.

MEET SOLO TRAVEL'S LITTLE SISTER: SMALL GROUP TRIPS

I told you earlier in this book that I was going to make a case for group travel and, well, here we are. If you don't feel fully ready (or wanting) to venture off completely into the unknown by yourself, I would like to highly recommend that you take a small group trip. And I'm not just talking about a day trip or a museum tour. I'm talking about a multiday group experience.

I know, I know. You might instantly recoil at that idea. "Isn't that the exact opposite of solo travel?" you might ask. And in some ways, you'd be right. You're surrounded by other people. You're not necessarily always picking your own places to eat and things to do. A lot of the logistics are decided for you. This may seem like the antithesis to going alone.

But really, small group trips are kind of a sister to solo travel. Emotionally, if you sign up for a group trip by yourself, you are still very much on your own. The people you're traveling with are still strangers (at least initially). Many small group trips leave time for solo exploration, so you'll still have plenty of moments of isolated wandering (if you want them).

Note a very important distinction here with my use of the word "small." It used to be that most small group tours didn't exist. One of the only ways to travel in a group was on a bus with fifty to seventy-five other people who were forced to follow well-trodden routes and dine in large, touristy restaurants. For someone seeking a solo travel experience (which often consists of some amount of blending in and eating locally), that probably seems pretty far from the ideal.

But now, group travel can be one of the *most* locally oriented ways to travel, because many travel companies offer small group tours, which some of us call "solo travel in a group."

Imagine this: You book a trip on your own and join between five and fifteen other strangers. Because of your small group size, your guide (who is local to the area) can take you into a tiny hole-in-the-wall restaurant, or have you sit down at a local weaving co-op and chat with the staff there, or go on a hike. You can be walking to a destination and decide as a group to veer off course to make a quick shopping trip to the local market. And, at the same time, you've got someone who can give you all the details about the history of what you're seeing, the origins of what you're tasting. You're getting up close and personal with a place, and you didn't have to plan any of it.

It's possible that you never considered any of these types of travel—a group experience, or a photography class abroad, or dinner with strangers—to be solo travel experiences. But they absolutely are. Maybe you've even tried some of them already. Maybe now you're starting to realize that you're a bit more of a badass traveler than you thought. Maybe you're not there yet— don't worry, you're perfect as you are either way. I'm not teaching you how to show up in a place by yourself. Anyone can do that. I'm teaching you how to make the absolute most of your journey. To see it with both eyes—and your mind—wide open. To taste every ingredient. That takes time, and practice. You can go on the same trip twice and experience it in two completely different ways. That's where the travel mindset comes in. We're going to help you get there.

IT'S ALSO OKAY TO BE LONELY

I realize that loneliness is getting a bit of a spotlight here, and it should, because a lot of us worry about it. Some of us don't want to be alone. Others of us very much *want* to be alone. It might depend on the type of person you are or the type of trip you want to take.

Many of the solutions above are geared toward taking a bit of the edge off of a solo trip, but it's also totally okay for your solo trip to have an edge. It is perfectly fine for that first solo trip to not feel perfect, or life-changing. Maybe it feels overly planned, or not planned enough. Maybe you feel anxious. It might take a few trips of varying levels of complexity for you to feel completely at ease with yourself. You might *never* feel completely at ease with yourself. All of those are possibilities, and they are all completely okay. Allowing yourself to sit in these places of discomfort—to go out for a delicious dinner by yourself simply because you want to and deserve to eat delicious food, even if you don't feel as confident as you're acting—is a critical part of travel, and of growth.

I still remember a story told by the late Evelyn Hannon of JourneyWoman, known by many as the world's first female travel blogger. She told it during her keynote at our first WITS Travel Creator Summit. She talked about how her first solo trip consisted of her crying on a park bench in Belgium all weekend, grieving after her divorce. Solo travel might look like that, too.

You might feel lonely even if you didn't plan on it. Not many of us are used to taking much time outside of our home comfort zone and without anyone around to share it with. Signing up for a group activity, going on a walking tour, or attending a Meetup might be a way to get around that, but you also might consider taking some time to write to yourself, or buying some postcards and writing them to friends and family back home. Sit with that discomfort, and take a minute to examine it. Why do you feel this way? What makes you feel uncomfortable about being with yourself? What are you learning about yourself in the process? In a future chapter I'll also introduce you to your new best travel friend, which will help you navigate these feelings a little bit more tenderly (and no, it's not a vibrator).

TRAVELING ALONE MEANS FINDING PEACE WITH OURSELVES

I would like to say that traveling alone starts with loving ourselves, but it doesn't have to start with anything. You don't have to love yourself to travel alone. You don't even have to like yourself. You might have started this journey of solo travel simply because of one of the reasons listed at the beginning of this chapter—that you were left behind, broken up with, or canceled on. Maybe someone backed out on you at the last minute and you're hoping to muster up the courage to get out there anyway. You might shrink at the idea of having to eat a meal in a restaurant on your own or navigating your way from the airport to your vacation rental. You might be traveling alone not because of a love of yourself, but *despite* yourself. It's okay to start from that place, too.

In reality, society hasn't given women a lot of opportunities to just love ourselves for who we are. For centuries we have been second-class citizens (if citizens at all), expected to be subservient to men or to our children. Only in recent history has that narrative been subverted, but still in many ways it persists in our subconscious. It's not a coincidence that even Sarai Sierra was shamed for traveling alone as a mother, as if she had a duty to bring her family along with her wherever she went.

That's why I want you to start your trip from a place not necessarily of self-love but at least some degree of self-acceptance and peace. Yes, it's not often that we're encouraged to be alone and happy. It might even feel downright uncomfortable at times. But as we talked about earlier, if there's any part of a solo trip that you should really lean into, it's those moments of discomfort—because that's where the growth really begins.

PEELING BACK THE LAYERS

In February 2018 I traveled to Tel Aviv on my own for an entrepreneurship retreat. I left my husband and my daughter, Nora, who was eleven months old, behind. The guilt that I felt leaving her was beyond any guilt I had experienced before, and the emotional (and, as a nursing mother, physical) discomfort was an understatement. But something inside me told me to go on this trip anyway, so I did. I cried the whole way there.

When I arrived in Tel Aviv, I had a day to myself before my program began, so I took a free walking tour around the old city of Jaffa, an ancient part of Tel Aviv with literally thousands of years of history. The group spent time wandering through Jaffa's winding passageways, learning stories of biblical history and examining regional architecture.

The tour dropped us off at the Jaffa flea market, and it was like the solo traveler in me took over. I wandered the market square and ordered a cappuccino. I traipsed through winding residential alleys and brushed my hands over stone walls. I sat and people-watched for hours. I found peace with myself. It was like I was meeting myself again for the first time, freed from the context of my home environment, my identities as wife and mother.

Our identities exist so deeply within the context of our geographic location, our home culture, and our friends and our family that sometimes they can feel nearly inseparable from who we are on the inside. So much of our surroundings shapes us—and many of those things are wonderful. I love being a wife and a mom. I love being a friend, a boss, a neighbor. But something about taking this trip on my own also gave me the freedom to meet the person who was underneath all those layers and to give time and attention to her and her needs.

Traveling alone isn't just something we do; it's a gift we give ourselves. For those of us for whom travel lives in our blood, the act of traveling alone is an act of self-care. We don't need to do it all the time, but when we *do* do it, we commit to it. It's a moment for us to prioritize ourselves and our needs. It's a chance to make ourselves better people by having experiences that cause us to learn and grow. It's an opportunity to take a breath, a pause, a refresher from daily life, and examine what it is that we want out of this one beautiful and complicated world. And that moment to take a step back and reconnect with ourselves—is the greatest gift of all.

On "Finding Yourself"

Let's be honest: The idea of "finding yourself" is a double-edged sword. On the one hand, it's great to be able to take time to get to know yourself—to meet the person underneath your layers of contextual identities. But your trip doesn't have to be life-changing, and it certainly won't be perfect. Being alone in a different environment will almost undoubtedly teach you something about yourself, but you might not notice that something until you've returned home. Give yourself the freedom to relax, be in the moment, and take your trip as it is—not as a major quest to find your one true identity, but as a chance to just relish some "me" time.

THIS TRIP IS FOR YOU (AND YOU ALONE)

Perhaps the best part of traveling solo is that no one but you can tell you how to do it. It is your experience, and yours alone. Want to pick up five different types of prosciutto at the grocery store and eat them in your hotel room? Go for it. Want to hike Patagonia with a group of wild and adventurous women?

Knock yourself out. Want to live and work on a farm and help make goat cheese? Sounds *maaa*-velous (sorry, I had to say it).

When you give yourself permission to have these experiences and don't force or expect anything else out of them, you're taking that first step toward a life of self-love. You'll use these moments of solo travel to give yourself a little grace, to laugh at yourself more for your inevitable foibles, and to get to know the "you" that exists underneath all the layers of home, and friends, and family. You'll meet someone that you might not get to spend a lot of time with—the you whom you've been all along, the you who is constantly evolving and being—and you might realize she's actually pretty cool. Maybe even one day, you'll check in at that hotel, drop your bags on the floor, and when the receptionist asks you how many keys, you'll look right at them and, with a glint of amusement in your eye, you'll say, "One," and nothing else. No "just"; no explanation. Because one is everything you need.

Chapter 5

LEAVING THE COMFORT ZONE

*"I soon realized that no journey carries one far
unless, as it extends into the world around us, it
goes an equal distance into the world within."*

—Lillian Smith

LET'S HAVE A CONVERSATION ABOUT COMFORT.

For most of our lives, we're encouraged to seek it out. Comfort is a hallmark necessity of many of our clothes, shoes, furniture, undergarments, even tampons. For some of these items, it's an absolute necessity (try wearing an uncomfortable bra for more than two hours and you'll know exactly what I mean). Other times, it's a feature ("I love your heels!"; "Thanks, and they're *so* comfortable!"). Either way, we put a lot of value in comfort. When something is uncomfortable, we avoid it, or at least reconsider if we actually need it, if its other qualities redeem it in some way.

While the importance of physical comfort will follow you through packing recommendations and hotel reviews (read: never, ever travel with uncomfortable footwear), there's also a certain amount of *dis*comfort—that is, emotional and mental discomfort—that I believe is essential to a travel experience. Making the active choice to leave your comfort zone is the key difference between traveling and just going somewhere. By doing that, you're making the decision to try something new, to challenge former ways of thinking, to leave the familiar. Those are precisely the same things that will allow you to absorb new information, consider new ways of life, and allow for a truly transformative travel experience.

We've already talked about getting comfortable with the discomfort of being alone, and that's certainly one of the types of discomfort you'll experience, but there are other ways you'll find yourself challenged. Some of those will be rather surface-level (being surprised by the fact that you had to pay for your orange juice on that budget airline you booked), and others will hit much deeper (like witnessing a scam or encountering corrupt local law enforcement). As we discussed in chapter 3, there will even be times when you question if the discomfort you feel is normal and an important learning opportunity or a red flag from your gut signaling you to escape a situation. It may seem obvious here while reading this book, but when you're in the moment, "good" and "bad" discomfort can be more challenging to decipher.

Here are three other types of discomfort that you will likely feel in your travels, each of which we'll spend some time discussing:

- The discomfort of being new at what feels like everything
- The discomfort of your identity, and noticing how it fits (or doesn't fit) in the local culture; the discomfort of the local gaze as others notice you
- The discomfort of being exposed and adapting (or not) to local politics and systems

Each of these discomforts is unique in its own way, but of course each also intersects with the other two. Your discomfort as a new person is directly related to your unfamiliarity with the local culture and traditions; it may be heightened by people noticing you. But for the sake of simplicity, let's break down each type of discomfort first. Then we'll talk about what to do with them.

THE DISCOMFORT OF BEING NEW

Not many other experiences make you feel like a newborn baby the way traveling to a completely new place does. First that discomfort might be cushioned by an overall feeling of wonder or awe: the moment when you first lay eyes on the Sydney Opera House or pull up to the majestic Bahá'í temple in Wilmette, Illinois. Even smaller moments will cause this: happening upon a gelateria with flavors you never imagined; seeing roasted insects on sticks at a night market; happening upon an ATM to pull out some cash and realizing you have no idea what the exchange rate is. Maybe you're driving on an unknown highway and feel confused about how the road systems work, or what exactly the traffic signs mean. There are hundreds of moments like this when traveling to a new place.

For many travelers, it's precisely this feeling—of being slightly disoriented or feeling so *new* to everything—that is exciting, a quintessential part of the travel experience. But that doesn't mean it's not tiring, too. When I first moved overseas, I napped a lot. My brain was constantly working overtime, adjusting to new experiences, translating from a second language, trying to pick up on social signals that weren't obvious yet to me. It's okay to give yourself the patience, and the space, to adjust. (Sneak peek: You'll also get one of my favorite tips for how to manage that in an upcoming chapter with what I consider my secret travel weapon, Day Zero.)

IDENTITY DISCOMFORT

Many of us—regardless (or perhaps because of) our race, ethnicity, physical ability, gender expression, sexual orientation, or other intersections—will at some point or another come to terms with how our identities may shift, or look slightly different, while abroad. This may be because we see ourselves in a new context and through a new lens. But it also may be because we experience, maybe for the first time, that unique feeling of *others experiencing us*.

There are numerous ways you might start to feel the local gaze, or rather, how others see and interpret you differently than you're used to, and that's especially true for women. It might be slight—like the way someone speaks to you (or doesn't speak to you) while you're waiting in line for a coffee or the way someone looks you up and down on the street. It may be more pronounced, like someone reaching out to touch your hair—or ignoring your existence entirely. Or it could be largely systemic, reflected not just in how other people interact with you, but in the greater local norms and customs, which may be presented as rules or laws, something we'll discuss in the next section.

These may be good things. I relished the way people prioritized me and gave me space in Belgium when I was pregnant with my daughter, moving so I had a seat, letting me cut to the front of lines. They might be neutral things, like the way children in rural Haiti brushed my skin and petted my arms, not having ever seen thick hair on the arms of a woman before. But they also could be negative, or even dangerous, like not being permitted access somewhere because of your gender, having your friendliness be misinterpreted as flirtatiousness or promiscuity, or being in direct violation of the law because you're queer. The reactions you experience might be in line with local culture and sentiments, developed through decades, centuries, even millennia of history that you may or may not be aware of. Or they could be independent acts of their own. You might not know right away.

Tahina Montoya, an officer in the US Air Force who is of Colombian descent, experiences this cultural dissonance all the time. "When I'm in the States, I'm too Colombian to be American," she explains, referencing how people interpret her presence, especially while in uniform. "In Panama when people asked me what I was, I would proudly say 'I'm Colombian.' People would say to me, 'You're not Colombian, you're American. Why do you want to say you're Colombian?' It had me question who I was on a whole new level."

What you do know is that when you travel, you're immersing yourself in a new place. But we're not just experiencing those places for ourselves. Those new places and the people in them experience us, too. Challenges we may deal with at home—racism, sexism, financial privilege (whether real or assumed)—may follow us into our travels, or they may present themselves differently. They don't necessarily just disappear because we're a tourist, though the things that make you feel different at home may be presented in a new light.

How we experience and interpret others experiencing and interpreting us can be unsettling, and sometimes uncomfortable. The constant whistle that followed me on the streets of São Tomé, and how when I told some male friends about how much the street harassment bothered me, they laughed and said that I was easily angered. The complete and utter embarrassment I felt when traveling through conservative southeastern Türkiye with the poor choice of wearing a dress that exposed my knees, knowing that I was making other local people visibly uncomfortable. The confusion I felt after eating dinner with my Portuguese family and retiring to the living room to play games, only to realize that all the women had stayed in the kitchen to clean up and were expecting me to do the same. In situations like these, we realize how much culture has played a role in our upbringing, in our self-understanding, and in our understanding of those around us, and how even the most basic things seem brought into question when we're away from home.

As a traveler, you can expect to be confronted with those feelings—the feelings of being new at everything and even experiencing familiar things differently—on the regular. What you might not be as prepared for is the fact that you are bringing something foreign to your destination, too: yourself. You might not be used to sticking out—or maybe you aren't used to blending in. Fact: You *will* look like a creature outside of its habitat. Some people won't know what to do with you. Others will try to categorize you with a "singles" meetup. We are uncomfortable with the idea of being alone and happy; of being at peace with our own selves, in our own solitude. But as we learned earlier, if there are elements of solo travel that give you that little pang of discomfort, those are exactly the places where you should start.

THE PRIVILEGE OF BEING AN OUTSIDER

For all that travelers often hope to blend in, there is often a real privilege in being an outsider as well, especially when it comes to women. There are times that you may find yourself given more access, or fewer restrictions, than local women simply because you're not from there. Maybe you'll find, for example, that your tour guide tells you that you don't need to wear a headscarf, even though all the other women around you are, or is a little more forgiving of your choice to expose your upper arms in a conservative area. These liberties may be racially coded: The expectation of your adherence to certain policies may be different in Morocco, for example, for a blond, white woman than for a brown or ethnically ambiguous woman, even if they both grew up on the same block in Oakland, California. If you are indisputably not from a place, you may find yourself with more flexibility in complying with local gender norms because locals know that you're not from there.

But our identity as women when we travel also runs the other direction: Sometimes we have the ability to unlock access to traditions and experiences that *are* private to women. A friend once told me a story about visiting a rural community in Nicaragua. She was the only woman traveling in her group and was pulled aside by some local women to experience a special women-only party honoring a fifteen-year-old girl who got her period. In some ways, we traveling women get the best of the best—a unique look at women's true experiences around the world and the ability to surpass a lot of the gender norms that limit women locally. To be able to do that, and for local communities to give us the permission to see into their world, is one of our biggest privileges.

We also, for better or worse, often are perceived as "safer" for *other* people to meet and talk to. You may find other travelers, and even couples, approaching you to talk with you when you're alone more than if you were with a friend or a group of people. In our "vulnerability" we may believe we're welcoming more negative attention, but we're also attracting new friends because we're considered a lot less intimidating. In this way, our identity as women is a superpower.

POLITICAL AND CULTURAL DISCOMFORT

In 2006 and 2007 I lived abroad in Coimbra, Portugal. Those days were filled with morning espressos by the riverside, afternoons studying Portuguese Manueline-style architecture, and late nights listening to the beautiful lyrics of traditional Coimbra fado. It was my true first time overseas by myself, hitting me in places that I didn't realize I had left completely exposed.

As a Portuguese American, visually, I fit right in. I got a "Euro-style" haircut (in this case a super angled and layered piece that verged on a mullet but looked *muito giro*), shopped exclusively at Zara and Bershka, and acquired some cheap sunglasses at the local market. No one was any the wiser I wasn't actually from there, and in many ways, I felt a lot of pride in that. Growing up as a little half-Portuguese kid in rural New Hampshire, I didn't have a strong sense of how I fit in ethnically. Was I Hispanic? Technically, the Portuguese originated in Spain. Was I brown? I had plenty of people throughout my life—some perfect strangers—announce to me that I should be proud of my brownness. Yet the paleness of my skin defied that. It was like we had all forgotten that it was in fact the Portuguese who were instrumental in the Age of Discovery, a misnomer for an era of cruel violence and colonialism.

But showing up in Portugal, wow, I felt so seen for the first time. Here were people who looked like me—ladies with soft bellies and chin whiskers who seemed to unlock this one missing piece about who I was, shedding light on years of confusion (like, you know, why I was the only girl I knew who had to shave her little mustache). The feeling was unexplainable. I had found the place I belonged.

Until I opened my mouth.

I cursed my American accent for giving me away whenever someone asked for directions, or what I would like to eat, or if they could assist me with anything. Not only did I feel "outed" as a foreigner, but my status as an American immediately opened me up to other conversations and questions.

"Ah, you're American," they'd say. And without hesitation: "So, what do you think about Bush?"

If you remember, George W. Bush was the US president at the time, and a good portion of the international community was displeased with some of his recent political decisions. As an American living abroad, I found myself confronted with an identity I didn't expect. While I thought I'd be embracing my Portuguese side, mastering the recipe for *pastéis de nata* and expertly shopping for good olive oil, instead, I became confronted with…well…my *American*ness.

Suddenly, without any preparation at all, I became a representative of my country. I would be asked questions about American current affairs and, many times, felt completely unprepared to answer them. I wished someone had prepared me for the barrage. Every time Bush decided something, it was like I was expected to explain everything on behalf of the United States, whether or not I agreed with every decision he made. I wondered if I should have gotten a political science degree, just to be able to explain the nuances of my own country.

This experience went beyond politics. When I travel abroad, people love to take me to McDonald's or serve me giant portions of watered-down coffee, because that's the America that they see and know from the movies. I have had countless moments when I'm really trying to work on my command of the local language and yet the person on the other end of the conversation absolutely insists on speaking English, or asking me about celebrity culture (another thing I know almost nothing about).

I explain this because up until this point in the book it does seem like as a solo traveler you become a master of your universe. You decide where you go, what you do, what businesses you support, what stainless steel water bottle you use, et cetera. And it's true that as a traveler you get to make a lot of your own choices (that's the whole point of traveling alone, right?). But the point of this chapter is not to cement the belief further that you get to do whatever you want. Rather, it's to help you understand that even when you make all these choices, there is still a part of your travel experience that you will not be able to control (at least not as much). And that part consists of what everyone else thinks of you, expects from you, and presumes to know about you already.

When you arrive in a new place, you're not just arriving there as you. You're arriving there with the history of people who looked or identified similarly to you who were in this place before you and whatever the media portrays about what your current culture is like now. You may be unique (and you are!)— but people will inevitably form biases about you based on the limited information they know about people who look like you. You might know what those biases are (after a while the Bush questions didn't surprise me, nor did the enthusiasm about hamburgers). But other times, you're going to walk right into another culture's embedded biases without knowing exactly what biases they have.

The phenomena of someone else experiencing you might sound a little awkward (voyeuristic even?), but there's an important context here that we need to address before we spend any more time on this subject. It's a topic that is really uncomfortable for some, but as you know well now, it's the uncomfortable topics that hold truth and power—the uncomfortable topics that we need to spend more time leaning into and working through. That topic is about the act of travel being inherently political in nature.

Most travel advertisements, shows, and media focus on the perspective of the traveler, as if when we travel to a place we are "discovering" a new destination behind a protective screen or glass. We sit in a rustic café in Jackson Hole, Wyoming, and watch scenes of people walking by with big cowboy hats or shoulders laden with ski equipment, like we've got front-row seats to a cool 4D travel experience, then disappear into our hotel rooms, unnoticed. But that assumption—that no one has noticed you, that you were simply an observer, that you're invisible—that's not true. Your very presence has an effect wherever you go, whether you like it or not.

We create that effect in a variety of ways: We impact an area environmentally by what we consume and how we choose to travel there. We make an impact financially by what we purchase and whom we purchase from. But we also make an impact sociopolitically, simply by choosing to be in this place at all. When we travel to a place, we—knowingly or unknowingly—embed ourselves in hundreds if not thousands of years of history that have shaped current sentiments and culture. We economically feed policies that we may or may not agree with simply through the taxes we are paying on goods and services. We support businesses that may or may not have values aligned with ours. We are the recipients of painstakingly wordsmithed travel messaging in our marketing materials and guidebooks.

Sometimes, if it's important enough to us, these political discomforts weigh heavily on deciding whether we even go on a certain trip at all. We might opt out of a trip to a certain location because we're afraid of unintentionally supporting a radical agenda or giving power to a corrupt local government's policies. That's a really tough decision to make—do you visit a place anyway, knowing that you might be actively contributing to something that you feel morally opposed to? On the one hand, there is not one place on the planet that is perfect, and this could be a great opportunity to learn about and support the local organizations that are doing the work to create change. On the other hand, there are thousands of amazing places to visit in the world—so maybe it's just not worth your energy to mull over this one. Once you start going down the rabbit hole, it seems like where you go—and what you experience there—embodies an endless series of ethical questions and dilemmas.

DISCOMFORT IS A CRITICAL PART OF TRAVEL

Here's the tricky part: No matter how many times you try to make the "right" choice on a trip—choosing a particular method of travel or opting in or out of a particular destination—there are certain discomforts that you will never be able to avoid. Some you'll learn to deal with, or even work around. Maybe you didn't know that public restrooms in Greece cost money, and after one too many moments when you desperately had to pee and didn't have change on you, you learned to carry some around for emergencies.

But there will be other times when you're confronted with something that you feel is morally wrong, and the tough pill to swallow will be that you, as a temporary visitor to this place, will probably not be able to change it. You will likely not be (nor should you be) responsible for any major cultural shifts during your trip. You might be heartbroken seeing so many stray dogs in your new city, but it also may not be your place to criticize the entire city for animal cruelty. You also have very little context regarding what steps have been taken and what has been accomplished so far (for all you know, the stray population has declined 90 percent from what it was, marking impressive progress rather than shameful negligence). The key point here is that you just don't know.

Making and holding space for the uncomfortable—and for the inevitable decisions that follow with that discomfort—is a lot to unpack. You may not feel ready to unpack it now. You may not feel ready ever. But the minute you open your suitcase, those uncomfortable moments are going to dive right in and make themselves at home. They're going to snuggle up to that travel-size tube of toothpaste and those compression socks. They are here to be part of your travel adventure because that's one of the fundamental components of what travel is.

So if they're going to be taking up space in your suitcase, we might as well talk about how to deal with them (and possibly even unpack them, too).

SO...WHAT DO WE DO?

Sometimes we talk about travel as a way to experience walking in someone else's shoes, and while travel does give us glimpses of that, believing that your own travel experience is an accurate taste of someone else's real life is misdirected. Your social location and identity will always influence the way you interpret the world, because the world is not a stagnant place to be interpreted one way. Your experience with a destination is heavily influenced by the people who live in it and have built it over time. Those people are often subject to biases and prejudices of their own. Their society may have been shaped by white supremacy and male dominance. It's why you and your friend may go on the exact same solo trip to the exact same place but leave with two completely different takeaways, depending on what you look like, what abilities you have, how much travel experience you have, and other qualities that make up your personal risk profile.

What travel does give you, however, is an intimate look at

how another community lives. That look may result in some personal reflections and an opportunity to examine inward. *What privileges have I been afforded in my home city or country that women in this place don't receive? What privileges do other women here have that my home community could benefit from?* Or maybe it has nothing to do with a place's treatment of women at all. Maybe you're awed by another place's technical advances, or public transit system, or cleanliness, or dedication to history, or food. Maybe you're amazed about the way a community cares for its elderly or the way a certain town uses solar power and composting to exist almost entirely sustainably. How a place uses geothermal energy to create a thriving tourism economy and support its farmers.

Other times, these discoveries are a lot more complicated and cause a greater ethical dilemma. You might encounter something that directly conflicts with one of your core values. The way a child or an animal is treated. Exposure to extreme poverty and the fact that no one else seems to be bothered by it. An encounter with a human rights violation that you know would not be tolerated at home and yet seems pervasive here. What do you do? When should you surrender to local culture, and when should you stand up firmly for your convictions?

The answer to this question is personal, and the line is sometimes fuzzy. It often comes down to an algorithm of factors—not just how important the issue is to you but how easy it is to speak up, how safe you feel, how urgently you believe you must address it, how likely it is that you'll receive a positive outcome, and how much you care about what outcome you get. You may encounter something important but not feel the need to urgently address it or not feel that you're in a position to say something. Or you may say something, but it might not change anything. All of these are possibilities.

Sometimes adages like "When in Rome, do as the Romans do" have been taken out of context over the years, but this particular phrase has pretty much held its meaning since it was first uttered by Saint Ambrose to Saint Augustine as a word of advice in AD 400. When visiting Rome, it's best to adapt yourself to the local customs and practices of the Romans, Saint Ambrose said. It's not just about fitting in or being undetected, as it was for me in Portugal. It's also about embracing another's way of life. Over the years, we've uttered this phrase in our favor. "When in Rome!" we announce happily when surprised with a sixth course that we didn't expect at a restaurant in Kyoto or when we're invited into an impromptu dance party at a quinceañera celebration in Mexico (even though in both cases we are quite far from Rome itself). Usually we say it when going with the flow works in our favor, like when Pope Clement XIV famously offered it as a reason for assuming a habit of regular afternoon naps in 1777. We don't often comment casually, "When in Rome!" if we are going along with something that we inherently dislike.

But should you? When should you embrace the uncomfortable and the unknown and just "when in Rome" it? When should you stick to your intuition even if you're at odds with the local culture? When is it okay to settle into a natural feeling of discomfort, because you're a traveler and discomfort is something you have to get really good at, and when should you be true to yourself and your needs? A few guiding questions may help you decipher when to do which:

Does This Violate My Core Values?

Of course, this is a loaded question. You may feel fundamentally offended by the way that store owner talked to women, but you might equally decide it's not worth your time and energy to go to bat over it. Not only should you ask yourself if your values are violated, but what resources and space you have to speak up and what alternatives are available. Maybe you've thought about the recent law that was implemented in your destination and you simply can't bring yourself to visit it, knowing that you're supporting a government you're morally against. These choices are not small, and it's up to you to determine how important they are to you, how urgent it is that you address it now, and how much you want to take on the emotional labor of saying or doing something.

For Kareemah Ashiru, founder of Hijabiglobetrotter and creator of the popular Facebook group Muslimahs Who Travel, speaking out and communicating her values in a polite way has been a critical part of having a positive solo travel experience. "When I lived in Spain, I realized that the way to greet is different from the US. They greet with *besos*, which is kissing. I wasn't super comfortable with that. I just had to explain to them that I'm not trying to be disrespectful, but I wasn't comfortable with that kind of greeting. Then I would opt for shaking hands or something else, to show that I was friendly and not trying to be disrespectful to their culture." She admits that it's not always easy, but when it comes to your core values, it's important to ask for what you need. "I try to be more vocal about the values that I uphold and some people question it, but many, many will respect it," she says.

Is There a Learning Opportunity Here?

If a traveler has one job, it is to visit a place with an open mind. So many parts of travel are about stepping outside your comfort zone, thus seeing or doing things you might not have known or considered before. The confusing part is, even things that feel like solid core values may shift over time with more exposure to the issue and the people affected. You may realize there are more components than you had considered or see someone else's perspective differently than you did before. Perhaps you'll have a chance to meet someone whose lived experience will show you that their way of life is actually okay, even nice. Rather than sticking to your ways, consider that you may be encountering a learning experience or an opportunity to engage local people in meaningful dialogue about the reality of their lives, even if that reality may seem impossible to fathom right now.

Can—and Should—You Change Anything?

There's a chance you will find that there are moments during your trip when, to your core, you feel that the culture you are visiting is doing something wrong. It could be a small thing (like being slightly disturbed that people are holding their forks differently than you do or don't use forks at all). It could be a big thing. It could be a fundamental ethical value that you hold very dearly. It could be a political right that is refused or a way certain people are treated or even ostracized. It may feel impossible to condone it or even ignore it, but at the same time there may be little else you can do in your short time there as a traveler. All cultures have been formed over centuries of refining—yours included. You will not be able to override anyone's culture in one week or even one month. Nor is it necessarily your place. Cultures of white saviorism and misguided volunteerism have on many occasions caused more harm than good, because outsiders believed they knew better than the locals about their countries or cities. Remember, the locals in your destination might have a few notes about wherever you live, too. There is a hard, uncomfortable, and unpleasant coming to terms with the fact that if we still choose to travel to a place, we must, at least on a certain level, accept it for what it is.

The Exception: When You Are in Direct Danger of Harm

We put so many expectations on ourselves as travelers to be open and to experience new and uncomfortable things. There is always, however, a line. There is a difference between learning or trying something new—that "good" discomfort—and putting ourselves in risky situations that could cause us harm. If you are approaching a line that involves your safety in any way, you must trust your gut, even if that gut is imperfect. That might include:

- Politely excusing yourself and taking a minute to separate yourself from the situation and breathe (or, depending on the context, running away in a full-on sprint)
- Asking for the help of a trusted friend, a tour guide, or even a stranger
- Calling an emergency number or crisis line
- Standing your ground, saying "No," and asserting yourself

I have spoken with hundreds of travelers and their advice always comes down to this: There are times when you must simply choose your intuition, because it's all that you have.

Is There Someone Else in a Better Position to Help?

If you find yourself coming to grips with something that feels completely wrong to you, chances are there are people who live in that place who feel the same way. Rather than spending your time and energy trying to change a local community that isn't yours, find a way to support (especially financially) local people who are already doing the work. These may be formal entities like LGBTQIA+ organizations or animal rights groups. While certain moments of discomfort may motivate you to take action while overseas, take a step back and think critically about whether you're the right person for the job. Supporting an existing effort and helping fund initiatives that are already on the ground are the best ways to help an important cause gain momentum, because those players already have a deep understanding of cultural context and the tools to make long-term change. As Zi of Pink Coconuts mentioned, every place has safe spaces and communities that you can tap into. You just need to find them.

READING SOCIAL CUES

So much of travel appears to rely on picking up on embedded social cues. The faster you can pick them up, the easier it seems to be to get around more smoothly. You'll notice that expectations about women are different in different places. Some places experience higher rates of gender parity, where women regularly contribute to the economy. In other places, women are still considered second to men and can't move freely without a chaperone. Our role as women travelers is in constant flux. We are almost always adapting to our new environment.

This is a complex enough conversation for me, a straight, mostly white woman visiting a new place, but is more complicated for queer women, women of color, non-neurotypical women, or any woman who sits outside of that mythical norm that we now know and understand so well. Because many underrepresented communities are used to having to read social cues more acutely for their own survival, traveling can be that much more difficult, especially when you're on your own and need to pick up on these social cues for yourself.

LGBTQ+ relocation expert Jess Drucker explains this experience really well. "There are different cultural cues that someone's gay in different countries, based on how people dress, how they act, how they're perceived, and then also what they know, culturally, or how they think about gay people or how often it might occur to someone there that someone's gay," she said to me.

These cultural cues help us navigate our own society, but when the cues are different in a new place, this dissonance could lead to confusion (both our own as well as that of others around us) or even aggression. This is particularly true when thrown in sharp relief with a sexist, chauvinist, or homophobic attitude—the straight man in the bar whose ego gets bruised by the gay woman who doesn't "want" him, for example, the possibility of her sexual orientation not even crossing his mind (and if it does, possibly resulting in aggression or violence).

"As an LGBTQ+ traveler, you are in an environment that is being influenced by you as much as you are by it," Jess explained. "When you're traveling out and being open, you may sometimes be forcing people to come face-to-face with a gay person in a way that they may not have to with their local population."

There are times when the way you're influencing another person will be unavoidable. But there are still decisions that you can make about what you do next. Zi Piggott of Pink Coconuts invites questions and uncomfortable encounters as long as they're delivered in respectful ways but also recognizes that it's a job that not everyone should have to fill. As an advocate, Zi believes that a key part of helping support that next generation of travelers is in inviting more exposure today.

"The reason why there are issues is because they weren't exposed to things and they don't know how to navigate them," Zi said about the people who often ask her questions about her identity as a queer non-binary person of color. "It's a chicken-egg problem. If people aren't visible, then people can't get used to you. But in order to be visible, you'd have to be uncomfortable, because you're going to have to stand out. When more people do that, it will become more normal. That's why I continue to tell people to travel, and to not compromise on their queerness. So that five years down the line, [when] another Black queer person comes through, it's going to be normal." For Zi, travel isn't just about exposing yourself to new places. It's about letting yourself be open so others can learn from you, too.

While adapting to new places might feel new to some, for others it's something they've had to do their whole lives. "I feel actually sometimes it's easier to adapt to new cultures and places as a neurodivergent person, because our whole lives we've had to train ourselves on how to observe and react in social situations very analytically. Which gives us the analytical skills to learn new cultural norms," explained trans and neurodivergent travel creator Kayley Whalen. "Plus, I definitely enjoy researching new cultures, and can get very excited about being in a new cultural context where different rules apply, and where in many ways people appreciate the effort I put into learning their culture, rather than assuming I know the rules already. You get credit for trying in a new culture, rather than [being] constantly shamed for failing in your own culture."

To Kayley's point, you shouldn't always prepare for the worst. Yes, there will be times when you feel truly challenged; there will be other times when you realize that aspects of who you are or experiences that you have been through in your life have prepared you better for these moments of discomfort and learning than you had thought. I cannot tell you how you are supposed to feel when you come face-to-face with an ethical conundrum, a moment of discomfort, the experience of someone else's prejudice or bias. I can only prepare you for the fact that these moments happen, and they're a very real part of our travel experiences. They're one of the many layers of why it can be so hard for people to distill the multitude of thoughts and experiences they had into a thirty-second "So, how was your trip?" summary at a party. There's what you experience on the outside, and then there's what you experience on the inside, which has a ten times greater impact on your thoughts and what you take away from your trip.

I wish I could give you all the magical tools so that you can navigate your solo travels with ease, but then I would rob you of all the beautiful and difficult ways you will learn and grow yourself. That little piece of discomfort that will snuggle into your suitcase and make itself cozy for the entire length of your trip? You'll learn how to deal with it. You'll even come to expect it. You'll take it home and it will influence the way you look at your whole life, your whole world, adding a new filter to things that once looked the same to you. You'll try to fully unpack it and then you'll find it again on another journey, ready to challenge you in new ways. You'll realize that this little piece of discomfort has become a part of you and that, in a way, you've come to embrace it, because it's precisely these moments of discomfort that have shaped you and made you into a fuller, more enriched person. They've challenged you to better understand what matters to you and who you truly are.

Chapter 6

HOW TO TRAVEL BETTER

"What one does when faced with the truth is more difficult than you'd think."

—Diana Prince

WHEN WAS THE LAST TIME YOU HOSTED A REALLY GOOD houseguest?

Maybe it was an old friend of yours who was visiting from out of town. Maybe it was someone you didn't know particularly well—a friend of your partner or your best friend's daughter who needed a place to stay while she was visiting colleges. Maybe it was your brother, whom you didn't expect to be a particularly tidy guy but who then ended up being really considerate and thoughtful.

What was it about the experience that made them an especially great guest? Did they come with a gift—a locally made snack or a souvenir from home? Did they offer to make dinner, using a recipe they learned at home, or maybe they were the first one up making coffee for everyone? Were they mindful of talking loudly on their phone or making noises in their room? Did they clean up after themselves, being careful to strip the bed and throw the sheets in the washing machine before they left?

Maybe you haven't had a houseguest in a while, but maybe you've been one. You came with a plant, spent quality time with your host, treated them to a meal as a thanks for the hospitality. At some point, someone probably gave you some advice about how to be a good houseguest, or you saw the activity modeled while growing up. But you might not have quite the same exposure to travel—that is, no one really formally introduced you to the concepts of how to be a good traveler. As adults we're expected to just jet off to another person's country having no idea how to make good choices not just for ourselves, but for the place we're visiting, too.

Being a good traveler is similar to being a good houseguest. That's because when we travel, we're entering someone else's home. But we forget that all too easily. When we research and read about places to visit we call them "destinations," as if they were created entirely for the purpose of our consumption. Too often we overlook the fact that one person's getaway is another person's everyday life. Your destination isn't just a place to visit. It's someone else's hometown. Your resort stay is someone else's livelihood.

The global tourism industry is the world's largest industry, making up 10 percent of jobs worldwide.[1] Some countries' entire economies depend on it. For better or worse, the decisions that you make as a traveler have a direct impact on someone else's—and oftentimes *many* people's—real life. There is a very serious disconnect between the experience of the traveler and the experience of the resident, and that comes from an inherent clash in desires and expectations. We don't feel the responsibility to make these decisions ethically, but we're also not really encouraged to, either. Those of us with passports carry an overwhelming privilege to see the world—a privilege that not everyone has (that's why it's called a privilege, right?). And because we have that privilege, it means that we have an additional responsibility to make better choices when we travel in order to afford the same opportunities to the people who follow after us.

The choices we make can be distilled into three categories: *economic* choices, *environmental* choices, and *cultural* choices. We must use our dollars to economically elevate local communities and limit the amount of leakage that's happening there. We must be mindful of our environmental footprint so that we can leave places with minimal impact. And we must educate ourselves on the reality of what we're experiencing, to ask questions that dig deeper into the heart of travel, to explore a place in the context of its real history, and to elevate important stories. Responsible travel sits at the intersection of these three components: economics, environment, and culture.

Travel Is Not Always Freedom

While the freedom to travel is an enormous privilege, please do not forget that travel is not always for leisure, and it's not always an act of freedom. It can also be forced.

Approximately 3.8 million adults and 1 million children, 99 percent of whom are women and girls, are victims of forced sexual exploitation[2] and are often trafficked long distances to make it nearly impossible to get home.

Millions of people every year are displaced, whether seeking political asylum or refuge from harm. Many must sacrifice everything they own, throw themselves into life-endangering circumstances, and be regularly subjected to human rights violations and acts of violence. If they are detained, their treatment is not always fair or just. Children can be separated from their parents. People can be stuck in detention centers for years, only to be forcibly returned to their point of origin.

Many women are forced to travel because lifesaving medical care is not available to them at home, whether due to politics, infrastructure, or money.

These are just some examples. Travel isn't always freedom, and remembering the ways travel can harm us—and has harmed others—is important, too.

WHAT'S RIGHT IS RARELY EASY

Here's a story.

Diana was born in 1941. She was raised by women in a small archipelago, learning to solve problems through compassion and listening. She believed deeply in hearing people's whole truth, which eventually became her superpower.

After a foreigner landed in her tiny town, she was asked to escort him back home. What followed was an epic adventure, and an inevitable exposure to the greater world—one that was ridden with conflict, injustice, and inequality. She spent the rest of her life reckoning with this clash between her culture at home and overseas and fiercely believing in the power of good. It became her hero's story.

I'm not just talking about any Diana, of course. I'm talking about Diana, an Amazon woman born in Themyscira, whom many of us know today as Wonder Woman. Come on, you didn't think we'd get this far without a Wonder Woman reference, did you?

I didn't grow up enamored by superheroes, but my husband, Marvin, did. He always had his kid-size nose in a comic book. He knew all the intimate details and stories of every superhero—their strengths and their weaknesses. He loved what they represented—a world that was fair and that could be better for all of us. He found comfort in the fact that the heroes always won, even when it appeared they might not. And they always seemed to know what to do, like they had this powerful moral compass that could always point to what's right.

The reality is that as regular folk, we're not superheroes. While we may have a good sense of what's right and wrong, there are gray areas, too. We don't always know what to do, and sometimes even if we do know what to do, the "right solution" isn't accessible to us. The travel industry is extremely complex and includes so many different suppliers, distributors, and players. Knowing which players are operating ethically is about as convoluted as reading an ingredient list on the back of a box of cake mix ("flour...sugar...thiamin mononitrate?"). Even if you spend a ton of time picking a great hotel to stay at, how do you know for sure that the suppliers *they* hire are working ethically, too? How do you know exactly what their hiring practices are, or how much they're composting, or if they're involving the local community? To be able to know and answer all these questions perfectly as a consumer isn't just difficult; it's impossible. It's a giant puzzle that never stops, and it's unfair to expect any single traveler to have the time, or the energy, to know all of the right answers—or sometimes to even ask the right questions.

To make it easier for consumers, the industry tries to identify the ways they're doing "good" and to highlight those things. They use words like "sustainable" and "ethical" to describe their work. They get certified as B Corporations or they bring in partnerships and nonprofit subsidiaries. But without perfect systems of regulation in place, we run a high risk of greenwashing pretty much everything. Greenwashing occurs when companies make something look greener than it actually is; maybe by the images and symbols they use or by the way they talk about something. A similar but different example of this is ethics washing, when companies perform an "ethics theater" of statements standing up about topics of importance without actually doing anything about them (a good example is when companies posted a black square on Instagram with the hashtag #BlackLivesMatter, but without doing anything to financially support Black lives, address internal racism, or examine their corporate DEI practices and hiring principles). Both of these concepts point to an industry that tries to look more responsible than it is. The companies utilize signals and cues that tell our brains these are the better choices. And sometimes they are. But often it takes the savviest of travelers to be able to separate the truth from the exaggeration.

Let's also add to that the fact that right now, the way our systems are built, the more responsible choice is also often more expensive, more inconvenient, and harder to find. And in that way, we face the hurdle of the "right" choice also being the more inaccessible one.

Let's take the cruise industry, for example. It's been long criticized for its danger to the environment, and the emissions statistics alone of the cruise industry are abysmal. A study of cruises operating out of Dubrovnik, Croatia, found that a typical three-thousand-person cruise ship will emit over twice as much in emissions as if each passenger had taken the same trip in a car.[3] That doesn't include the amount of waste and air pollution that cruise ships create or the fact that their port visits rarely provide any meaningful investment in the local community (in fact, the UN World Tourism Organization, UNWTO, has cited that as much as 80 percent of tourism dollars spent in an area are funneled outside the country, a phenomenon called economic leakage,[4] and the cruise industry is consistently listed as the among the worst here[5]). And because many cruise ships operate in international waters, they can also avoid tax regulations and laws on fair work and wages if they so choose. Oh, and they harm marine life. So...there's that.

But here's the flip side: The cruise industry also does some incredible things in making travel accessible. For some, it's the only way they can afford to travel. A Carnival cruiser can take a four-day Caribbean vacation for just $269, or $67 per day. And that includes all the food you could eat. I remember my travel-loving grandmother, Margaret, who cruised well into her mid-nineties. At that point in her life, she wanted to see the world, but cruising was the only way she could physically do it with her mobility issues. Cruises make the world accessible to people who might not be able to travel otherwise, both physically and financially. They are also one of the few types of travel that multigenerational families can do easily. And we can't deny that they generate a *ton* of economic output and jobs, even after leakage. Does that make the cruise industry *all* bad? Things start to get muddled, right?

Just like purchasing organic, grass-fed, and sustainably

sourced beef, travel—and even cruising—can serve our communities and minimize negative impacts, but there's a price tag that comes along with it. That's because taking the extra effort to source sustainably also often means avoiding shortcuts, focusing on smaller (and therefore less operationally scalable) solutions, taking the time and energy to build local partnerships, and paying people fairly for their work.

The reality is, asking travelers to make perfectly conscientious consumer decisions is nearly impossible. There are just too many things to know and learn about and too many decisions to make.

"I would underscore a million times that conscious consumerism is not the answer," Kelley Louise, sustainable travel expert and cofounder of a global community and network called Impact Travel Social Club, said to me during a chat about what travelers can do to make better decisions. "Conscious consumerism will teach you about how you as an individual can make changes, but it inherently also places blame on you as an individual. We need to have that knowledge so we can go out and dismantle systems. But ultimately, it's not your fault. A huge part of our inability to have a sustainable experience and do it in a way that's easy is because of the way that the industry exists, the way that things are regulated, and the systems that we were born into. So we have to do things the best way that we can, but we also have to know that learning and making mistakes is part of the process. We were born into this imperfect system [where] we need to advocate to create change."

The interesting part of all of this is that travel is the medium as well as the solution. We need to travel to open our eyes to the changes that we can make. By being informed about ways to travel that are better for everyone involved—the travelers, the hospitality and tourism workers, the local community members, and most certainly the environment—we can equip ourselves with the information and the power to explore solutions for an industry that better serves all of us. But only if we do something about it.

WITH GREAT TRAVEL COMES GREAT RESPONSIBILITY

You may at this point be asking why you should care, and I don't blame you. You came here to learn about how to travel alone, not how to fix the entire world through your travels, right? But when you are confronted with the world while solo, things hit more deeply. Your vulnerability as a solo traveler means that you will experience your destination without the social buffer of a friend or travel companion; instead, it will hit you directly in the face. Being a true global citizen isn't just about checking off bucket lists; it involves caring about other people's homes, noticing the impact you have, and thinking of travel as a mutual relationship. Places do not exist to serve our needs and adventures and then disappear when we're not there.

Responsible travel is also a lot more popular than you realize. Sustainable tourism was valued at $3.3 trillion in 2022 and is projected to reach $11.4 trillion by 2032, increasing at a rate of 14 percent per year.[6] A study of 11,000 people conducted in February and March 2022 by Wakefield Research found that 90 percent of people explored sustainable options when planning travel. But they also found that 70 percent of people felt overwhelmed by starting the process of being more sustainable.[7] We might understand implicitly how important it is to make good choices, but when it comes time to make a decision, we buckle—because it's just really complicated. Part of the reason is because, as we discussed above, there are systems designed to fail us. But another part of it is simply that we don't have the tools to easily make responsible choices. So let's get some help.

INVESTORS IN OUR TRAVEL ECOSYSTEM: MINDFUL ECONOMIC IMPACT

How much money do you spend on travel? If you add it all together, even if you're traveling on a budget, it's a lot. The average American spends over $1,500 on a one-week vacation;[8] if you're traveling to an American city, you could easily spend two to three times that. The average boomer spends $7,800 on a trip and takes four to five trips per year.[9]

There are a million ways to slice it—do you drop $300 on a hotel or $30 on a hostel? Do you dine in an expensive restaurant or shop at the grocery store?—but at the end of the day, you're spending money—a lot of money, all at once. This isn't just buying a new toothbrush. This is food, lodging, activities, gear, plane or train or boat tickets (sometimes all three), or a rental car—it's an investment.

I want to use the word "investment" because we have to start thinking about ourselves not as consumers but as *investors*. An angel investor is a person who contributes money to the growth of a business. They give five or ten thousand dollars, sometimes more, sometimes less. And in exchange, the investor expects a certain amount of ownership in the business.

When we travel, we also spend a good chunk of money on the tourism ecosystem, and I want you to think about yourself as an investor in that space. An investor is not just giving money; they're putting money down on an idea that they think the world should see. They're choosing to become an active part of that idea, even if just financially.

Should we be much different, then, as travelers? Rather than thinking of ourselves as passive consumers of travel, we should instead think of ourselves as active investors. And when we start to think of ourselves as active investors, it changes the questions we ask. It's not always just about getting the best bang for our buck—it's about making choices that allow the travel industry to flourish in the way we believe it should, so that it can last for years to come. It forces us to think about investing in an industry that is regenerative, sustainable, and ethical; that adds, rather than detracts, from the places we visit so that we can be sure that those places are there for generations to come (I mean, we want a good return on our investment, right?).

We often call upon the travel industry to make changes, and it should. Cruises should find ways to be more environmentally sustainable. Tours should look for ways to avoid disenfranchising the communities they're visiting. But in the United States, we live in a capitalist society. For the most part, companies won't change unless the consumer demands it (or unless government forces it). And the way a consumer can demand something is through their spending. Every dollar is a vote. We must use our votes wisely.

Whenever you spend money, you might want to ask yourself the following questions:

- Who is receiving this money? What systems are in place to ensure that people are being paid fairly and adequately?
- Is there a better, more direct way I can be paying someone for their work, or is this a service that I am gladly opting into for convenience and ease?
- Am I supporting a business that I believe is doing good for its wider community and working to make this area better? In other words, is this something I want to invest in?
- What businesses or people am I *not* investing in because I am choosing instead to put my money into this particular business?

I realize that you're not going to have the time or the energy to pull out a list of ethical questions to ask yourself every time you buy *elote* from a street vendor or pay admission to a museum. It's probably why so many people find making responsible choices exhausting. But there are a few key points to consider that can help you decide where and how to spend your money wisely in a way that helps rather than hurts locally.

Here are a few ideas:

Shop Local

There's one thing you can pretty much find wherever you travel, and that's local businesses. These may be easier to find on a walk around town, like locally owned restaurants; or require a bit more research, like locally owned walking tours. If you don't know where to begin, the local tourism office can be a great jumping-off point, as they can direct you quite easily to which businesses are locally owned and operated, and connect you with people who can help you out. They can also be a great help in finding women- and minority-owned businesses, because they know their city better than, well, anyone (it *is* their job, right?). In fact, I'd recommend the local tourism board over an internet search pretty much any day when it comes to finding standout women-owned businesses. Doing a Google search for local bloggers and content creators, then looking up their favorite businesses and travel tips, is also a great way to get helpful information and feel like an insider at the same time.

Some other ways to invest in the local economy include:

- *Skip the tourist shop chains and seek out locally made souvenirs.* Those tote bags stamped with "**BARCELONA** BARCELONA *BARCELONA*" were likely not manufactured locally (if you don't know what I'm talking about, don't worry—you'll start to see them everywhere on your travels).

- *Take a cooking class.* This not only gives you access to local people and the opportunity to try local cuisine, but you also get to learn a skill that you can take home with you.

- *Hire a local photographer.* If you're planning on traveling alone, getting photos of yourself is going to be hard. Hiring a local photographer not only supports a local business but serves the double duty of getting you some amazing pictures of yourself (and can also be a great way to get the lay of the land from someone whose job it is to see a place in unique and special ways).

- *Incorporate your shopping with an experience.* Visit a winery and then buy wine to take home. Visit a coffee farm and buy a bag of beans.

Doing the Best You Can with the Information You Have

At home we can be a lot more conscious about our purchasing choices, because we are familiar with local policies and current events. We understand the challenges our home country or city is facing and we can choose to act accordingly. But when we're abroad, it's much more complicated. We are out of context, and it would take a lifetime to catch up.

If we want to make conscious purchasing decisions, we need to rely on shortcuts—lists from the internet, advice from local tourism boards, tips from local experts. Those shortcuts won't always work perfectly. Even tour guides have their own personal lens or filter, and adequate diversity and representation in the tour guide industry is still something being worked through, which means (again) that only a narrow perspective is often being represented and disseminated. We have to be okay with the fact that we are making the best decision we can with the information—and the time—we have.

Trade Your Sweat for Sangria

Ah, volunteering. The most lovely, wonderful, and magical experience you can have. You not only get to travel, but you also get to experience local culture and give back to a local community, right?

In theory, volunteering abroad is great. We share the amazing skills that we have, for free, with other people who need them.

The vast majority of us who volunteer do so because we want to use our services and skills to help others. That's basically the entire point of volunteering. But if we're thinking about traveling somewhere with the intention of volunteering there, we should evaluate this decision—and our following plans—extremely carefully.

There are a few reasons for this. First, travelers who volunteer abroad are very unlikely to be able to generate any sort of long-term, sustainable impact within the community they're volunteering in. While it may feel like even a few days or a week will help, using a series of volunteers ends up displacing a local worker who could have been paid for that labor, which could have helped them and their family, as well as the local economy.

Second, your volunteer experience does actually cost your local organization money. It may be in the form of time spent to onboard and train you, the cost of the marketing and coordination of the volunteer program, or even just the tools and materials you're given.

And, perhaps most importantly, volunteers may not actually be experts. Many volunteer opportunities give volunteers the ability to do work that they might not actually be qualified to do at home. This not only further perpetuates a culture of white saviorism and Eurocentrism—it's also potentially really harmful putting an inexperienced person into a role they're not qualified to do. At best, the job is set back from progress. At worst, people can get hurt.[10]

If you have an interest in volunteering abroad, I can recommend no better reading than Pippa Biddle's book *Ours to Explore: Privilege, Power, and the Paradox of Voluntourism*. In the book, Pippa classifies impact into two categories: inputs and outcomes.

When we volunteer abroad, we often think about inputs—what we can do to help. But really we should be thinking about outcomes—how our efforts translate into long-term solutions for the local community. If our efforts can't create long-term, sustainable outcomes, they're not worth it—*and* they completely disenfranchise and disable local communities, *and* they function only to make the volunteer feel good. By focusing your effort on long-term outcomes, you're in a much better position to see the full picture of your volunteer experience.

If you're determined to volunteer abroad, do your research and think about what you can offer. You might be more interested in getting your hands dirty and building a school, but offering your accounting skills to a local nonprofit or helping clean up their database with your web experience might be a more productive use of your and their time and energy.

In fact, sometimes the best thing you can do, instead of volunteering, is to just be a tourist, spend money, and support the local economy. Order a cocktail with freshly made, organic, local ingredients at a locally owned bar or restaurant. Hire a local tour guide to show you around. Stay at a bed-and-breakfast that contributes its profits to local social efforts or works toward net zero carbon emissions. By investing your money rather than your time, you're helping ensure that those dollars stay in the community you're intending to support.

Fight the Urge to Haggle

When I lived in São Tomé, I remember taking a motorcycle taxi that had two prices: one for locals and another for tourists. I was asked to pay the tourist fee, which was markedly higher, and at twenty-three years old, I was royally pissed. I felt like I was being deliberately taken advantage of, and this motorcycle taxi driver didn't even try to hide it. "You're not from here," he told me, "so you should pay more."

Looking back, I realize that he was right. While I don't think that tourists should be completely blindsided and stripped of all their cash, I also believe that if we can afford to pay more, we should. If anything, it's because we should be investing in places we're visiting, because we're not contributing much in the long term any other way.

While I do believe we should be mindful of scams and have a good understanding of how much something should generally cost (taxis are, to be fair, a place where you can easily be taken advantage of if you don't have any idea of the average fare, for example), I've stopped aggressively haggling, especially at local markets and with artisans, and particularly in places where the American dollar is stronger or where I have more financial privilege. I'm fortunate to be able to afford to purchase these items; if it's a difference of a dollar or two, whose livelihood will that affect more?

WHEN THE CANALS RUN CLEAR: MINIMIZING OUR ENVIRONMENTAL IMPACT

There have been times when I've wondered to myself, *Does it make better sense just to stay home?* A round-trip economy flight between New York and London emits as much carbon emissions as a person in Ghana is responsible for in a year.[11] Is our desire to see the world actually hurting it?

When we all stopped traveling in 2020, some magical things happened to our environment. According to the International Energy Agency, global emissions plunged by two billion tons, the largest decline in history—and half of that came directly from our driving and flying less.[12] The canals of Venice ran clear for the first time; fish populations in the Mediterranean began to recover. But a paper by Lauretta Burke, Mark Spalding, and Alan Fyall explained that it wasn't all good. Many destinations that relied on nature tourism suffered, and the economic losses of not having tourism gave way to illegal poaching, fishing, and deforestation, activities that nature tourism actually protected.[13]

We can agree that the carbon emissions from travel are bad, but many other parts of travel, such as the ability to support local business, to build awareness for natural ecosystems, and to support cultural exchange, are really good. I would hesitate, then, to pigeonhole travel into a "good" or "bad" binary. It is simply a method we use to see the world. And the important thing we can do is make sure that method exerts as much good, and as little harm, as possible when we do it.

This is the thinking that has led many members of our industry to the sustainable and regenerative travel movements. Sustainable tourism is the idea that we can leave the condition of places as good as when we arrived. This means reducing or offsetting our carbon footprints with a donation or employing reusable products. It's emptying the trash at your Airbnb and sweeping the floors before you leave.

Regenerative tourism is a step further. It's the idea that not only can we limit our footprint, but we can leave a place even *better* than we found it. Neither of these concepts is limited to just environmental impact; they also focus on helping grow local economies and preserving local culture. They can focus on highlighting traditionally underrepresented parts of the culture, like amplifying and elevating women- and minority-owned businesses or supporting a region's immigrant community.

At the end of the day, a trip that is good for the environment and for the local community often goes hand in hand with a trip that is more immersive, transformative, and fulfilling for the traveler. When you're thinking about your travel plan, keeping in mind both aspects will make for the magic combination.

So where do we actually find travel opportunities that are not just better for the world but more fun and fulfilling? Here are some places to begin:

Slow Down

The concept of "slow travel," where you take more time to explore and experience the place you're in, is having a moment, and the neat thing about it is that it also helps reduce that carbon footprint you're making when you jet-set around the world. Instead of knocking out three major sites in one day, try taking public transit and focusing on one thing at a time over three days. Swap out a bus tour for an e-bike or walking tour. Maybe instead of hopping an international flight home with multiple legs, you utilize the local train system to slowly work your way toward an airport with a direct flight, stopping along the way to marvel at the new places you're visiting on the trip and, when you're not stopping, just gazing out the window at the incredible views that you pass.

As a solo traveler, slow travel has some mental and emotional benefits, too. It puts less pressure on you to do everything perfectly and right. When I travel alone, I am more at ease when I know I have all the time in the world to figure something out. Not having a complex itinerary and letting myself travel at my own pace allow me to take travel hiccups and changes along the way with ease, and I can just enjoy my trip more.

While I'm not necessarily advocating for you to completely abandon air travel, and while I recognize that not everyone has all the time in the world to aimlessly meander, I am suggesting that, if you want to be an eco-friendly traveler, flying every week-end across the world might not be the best use of your carbon footprint (or your time). Slow down. Let yourself enjoy your destination. You might get a lot more out of it than you think.

Have an Adventure

Did you know that adventure travel is one of the segments of the industry that experiences the least leakage? What that means is when you pay for adventure travel activities, whether that's a kayak tour or a nature walk—you're likely investing money into the local community more than most other travel segments (about 76 percent of those funds, in fact).[14] Many adventure travel activities not only get you exploring the outdoors and seeing wildlife in its natural habitat, but they're also naturally predisposed to be more regenerative and eco-friendly (because without a robust natural environment, most adventure travel activities would lose their luster) and tend to involve local experts and community members the most. This is one of those natural travel ecosystems where a better travel experience for the traveler is fundamentally tied to a more responsible one, too.

Adventure travel itself need not be super "adventurous"— you don't need to be risking your life. Hiking, camping, kayaking, bird-watching, cycling, and, yes, even e-biking qualify in the adventure travel space. The idea is to spend more time outside, and in that way, connect with and build awareness of our natural environment in a meaningful way. If you're one of those people who've always wanted to ride an elephant but know about the harm that riding elephants does to the animal, try visiting a locally owned wildlife sanctuary. If you've dreamed of swimming with dolphins, go snorkeling.

Get off the Top 10 List

In 1833, British writer William Forster Lloyd coined the term "the tragedy of the commons." It describes a situation I learned about in business school that occurs when individuals act out of personal gain and ultimately hurt their greater society in the process. This may be through depleting a natural resource or, in the case of over-tourism, destroying the qualities that make a historic site, or even an entire city, special. If you visit the famous Mayan ruins of Chichén Itzá in Mexico, you'll see the tragedy of the commons at its worst: Because so many people wanted to climb its steps, the steps began to erode. Now, visitors are banned from climbing, in hopes this spectacular piece of cultural history can be preserved for generations to come.

If you've ever heard someone tell you not to visit Venice, you're probably already familiar with the concept of over-tourism. The city, with a population of 55,000 people, receives over 120,000 visitors—*per day.*[15] This has resulted in intense overcrowding; pollution (both through litter as well as the emissions and fumes from the city's many cruise ships); the physical destruction and erosion of stairs, walkways, and monuments; and, let's be real, the inability for anyone in Venice to get a job other than in tourism.

Over-tourism has hurt Venice in a deep way. But there's a problem with telling people not to visit Venice, and if you have small children like I do or at least have spent more than five minutes with a small child in the last ten years, you'll understand why. It's because if you tell a person not to do something, they become even *more* motivated to do it. And with more and more tourists knowing that Venice is being physically affected by its tourism, more and more tourists want to see Venice *while it's still there.*

I get it; places with depleting resources are getting higher on visitors' lists. While some cities took the great pause of COVID to make changes to how their tourism is run (in Venice, city officials implemented a day fee for visitors and set limits on the size of cruise ships that could visit), we as travelers should also take responsibility for our actions and be mindful of how our travels affect the places we visit.

Want to "live like a local"? The first thing you need to do is get yourself off the first page of Google. Immersive travel experiences are hard to find in "top 10" lists. While this might mean not visiting places like Venice at all, for others it might just be a matter of looking at Venice differently. Rather than spending a weeklong trip there, consider limiting your trip to just a couple of days or staying in nearby Chioggia ("little Venice") or Murano and taking a day trip in. There are ways to still see the sights without contributing to overpopulation, and in the process you can support other local tourism ecosystems that are often overlooked and thus truly excited to welcome you, giving you a deeper and more connected travel experience overall. It might take a little more research or more time or logistical savvy to get there, but you can (quite literally) spread the wealth and feel good that you're helping preserve some of those treasured sites.

Little Things Matter

While it may feel like traveling responsibly starts with making big, trip-altering decisions, sometimes it's the little things that seem to make the biggest difference when it comes to being a good guest. If we all were to practice these things, they'd add up fast and make an enormous impact. And they take very little work. For example:

- *Limit your waste.* Bring that reusable water bottle so you're limiting your dependence on single-use plastics. Take a foldable reusable bag with you, or carry a backpack during your day trips to hold any items you pick up along the way. Try not to order more food than you'll eat. (This one is really hard, especially if you don't know how much food you'll be served. Try just ordering òne plate at a time rather than requesting everything. Or ask to take extra food back to your hotel room and keep it in the minifridge.)
- *Go digital.* Get a travel guidebook from the library or buy one secondhand if you need paper. Use an app or a digital list if you want to eliminate paper use entirely. Take pictures of brochures and pamphlets and then put them back. Even if you intend to recycle your paper, it's still better to not use it at all.
- *Cut back on the souvenirs.* Souvenir purchasing is truly a black hole. You buy one thing, then you buy another. Then you realize you need to get gifts for people. Then you end up purchasing more than you can carry. When you get home you realize you didn't need half of it. Why did it feel so special abroad and then somehow lost its meaning as a gift? Try limiting purchases to one special souvenir for yourself, and plan in advance anything else you're getting. Don't buy for buying's sake. Buy things that will last and that you'll use or admire in the long term.
- *Skip the room cleanings.* If you're staying in a hotel for a day or

two, you should be able to clean up after yourself enough to not need housekeeping every day, right? Save the extra water, towels, and disposables that are replaced during a room cleaning.

- *Take public transit.* It's really easy to fall into the habit of Ubering everywhere when you're in a new place, and we'll talk about that when we discuss your Day Zero in a later chapter. But taking public transit can be one of the most immersive ways to travel locally, and it's a lot better for the environment than driving everywhere.

WHAT'S THE TRUE STORY? BEING A CULTURALLY AWARE TRAVELER

Onstage at a Wanderful event, a speaker asked us, "How many ignorant people do you know who are well-traveled?" She was making the point that well-traveled people are not ignorant, but I actually don't know if that's true.

Travel is an amazing medium; it's a tool that can be cultivated. It can teach you so much. It can make you a better person. But if you don't use it correctly, it can also do the opposite.

You might travel to a lot of places and see a lot of things, but if you're not asking the right questions, you probably aren't getting the right answers and stories. In fact, without the right lessons and context, you may use travel as a way to *reinforce* the biases you have, rather than to disrupt them.

In an article for *Lonely Planet*, Rosie Bell said this beautifully: "Travel can be a remedy for biases—conscious and unconscious," she explained. "Yet many limiting beliefs about 'others' are persistent even in those who are well-traveled.

Simply leaving one's home is insufficient to dismantle prejudices. After all, not everyone travels with their eyes open and others pack their biases around with them."[16]

Truly immersive travel doesn't just happen to us. It's not something we can simply opt in for and have presented to us like tickets to a show. It takes work. It's getting real with a place's true stories and history. And that history can be wildly uncomfortable. It doesn't mean just going to a luau in Hawai'i and marveling at its creative use of Spam. It means taking the time to learn about indigenous Hawaiian traditions and culture. It means understanding (at least to a degree) its more complex undertones: that it was taken over by the United States to be used as a military base, that its queen was arrested by US Marines at gunpoint and overthrown, and that this apparently quirky love of Spam actually came from an abundance of the stuff shipped to GIs in the 1940s.[17] Every place has stories like this if you take enough time to listen. While that luau might have been presented to you beautifully, it is up to you to learn to the best of your ability more about what you are experiencing. Otherwise, it becomes presentation without substance, part of a vicious cycle of tourist expectations and an economy that values culture for consumption; the same ugly ingredients that manifest themselves in cultural appropriation and the oversimplification, caricaturing, and ultimately disrespecting of someone's true lived experience.

Travel is rooted in the voyeurism of other people and places. There's no front door to a place (except maybe Passport Control); we simply enter without really knocking. No one invites us in. In a lot of ways, we feel entitled to see the world because we believe the world is "ours." And on the one hand, it is ours—we should all be equal citizens on this globe we occupy. But in other ways, we must recognize that we're entering spaces we are actually quite ignorant about. And because of that, we rely very heavily on the narratives that are served to us—narratives that are still predominantly delivered from and catered to a young white, male, "mythical norm" audience.

Getting to the root of these travel stories, then, is our responsibility. It consists not just of digging deeper into the real stories and history of places, but seeking out voices and perspectives that may not have been part of the traditional mainstream. It means understanding both the history of the past and what major cultural and political movements may have shaped it to be what it is, as well as the current dynamics and events that take place today. You must be open to all of this, because you cannot filter the experiences you allow into your travels and call that travel authentic at the same time.

An article called "Transformational Tourism as a Hero's Journey," published in the journal *Current Issues in Tourism*, outlines what's needed in order to achieve transformation in a tourism experience. This includes things such as the following:

- Doing unfamiliar activities
- Interacting with people
- Living in the moment
- Reflecting[18]

Basically, if you really want travel to make you a better person, you have to lean in to the experience of trying new things and immersing yourself in your new place. That is fully in line with our travel mindset. If you're not trying something new and getting uncomfortable, the lessons you could be picking up from your travel experience are falling short. That means venturing outside your hotel room and embracing how a place is different from your home.

Here are some other ways to be a more culturally aware traveler:

- *Read a history book.* It doesn't have to be a whole book. It could be a few articles. It could be some YouTube videos if you want or a podcast. It could be a memoir. In some cases, it could even be historical fiction. It's a great thing to do on the plane. Immerse yourself in the story and get to know the context of the place you're about to enter.

- *Question everything.* In the same breath, I encourage you to challenge everything given to you at face value. When you read a plaque, think about what might have been missed. Whose history was documented well enough that this story could be told? Who was left out? When you look at a monument, ask yourself, *Who could afford to pay for this and why?* Did you know that only 3 percent of historic statues in the world are of women?[19] Think about the thousands— millions—of stories that have gone unrecorded.

- *Connect with locals.* A great way to connect with the true current events of a place may be right under your nose in the form of a local community group—your local Wanderful hub, for example, or an expat-friendly Meetup group. There's a lot you can learn during one dinner with a group of locals to better understand what stories are being under-delivered and what stories are being completely missed.

- *Seek out the indigenous community.* Almost every place on earth has indigenous history, and many still have strong active indigenous communities. Remember that most of us aren't ever actually locals of a place—the majority of us emigrated from somewhere. Take some time to learn about, honor, and support the indigenous heritage of a place. It is the truest, closest human connection to the land you're visiting. Use a tool like the nonprofit Native Land Digital (native-land.ca) to learn more about the indigenous name of the place you're visiting and the tribes that are associated with that land. Ask your destination's local tourism board for information about the indigenous communities represented in your destination, or indigenous cultural centers or museums. Bring home a souvenir from an indigenous-owned shop.

- *Celebrate immigrant-owned businesses.* If you want to experience the richness of travel, order Chinese food in Jamaica or pick up some Greek cuisine in Japan. Get closer to the immigrant communities of a place—communities of people who have made a place an adopted home—in order to get a much more interesting and well-rounded perspective of what that place is about.

- *Be careful with your camera.* Digital cameras (and phones) have done a lot of great things for us, but they've also made us pretty trigger-happy. Sometimes we forget that we're taking pictures of real people when we capture memories, or that we're in sacred spaces. Before you take a picture, take a moment to really open your eyes to your surroundings. Make sure you retain them in your memory first. If you're taking a picture of a person, ask for their permission. Many cultures believe that photographs *of* them belong *to* them. Avoid taking pictures of children, no matter how cute they are. And take time to know what you're taking a photo of before walking on.

For me, travel is like food. There's food that hurts your body and food that nourishes it. You need to know a little bit about nutrition in order to know what's good for you, but if you eat well, it can sustain you for a lifetime. These lists may sound like a lot of homework, and in some ways, they are. "With great travels comes great responsibility," right? While you can't possibly know everything about a place or the right choices you should make to be a sound traveler there, making the effort makes a difference.

That said, as a traveler, you're going to consume things that aren't always good for you. Maybe it's because you just want a vacation, or you don't have the time or energy or budget to be extra-mindful of your travel habits. What's worse is that sometimes you're going to consume things that you *think* are good for you but actually aren't. Maybe it's a tour or a hotel that boasts itself as "sustainable" or "green" or "fair and ethical" but actually isn't. Maybe you'll know you made a mistake while consuming it; maybe you'll never know. Identifying the "right" ways to travel sometimes feels like a game where the earth is keeping score but you won't know what the score actually is until it's too late.

While at the end of the day this can feel overwhelming, it doesn't have to be. If you're struggling to figure out your most responsible move, ask yourself these questions:

- Who is being affected by my decisions, and do they have a voice in the matter?
- What stories are being told and what stories are being left out?
- How is my money affecting this place or this business? How

transparent is the business in their values, how they make decisions, and where my money goes?

- How lasting are the effects of my impact here (whether good impact, like investment in a local business doing important work, or bad impact, like the leftover waste I generated)?
- Would I want someone like me to be a guest in my home city or country?

The best travel experiences—best for you, best for the local community, best for the planet—aren't as disparate as you might think. And in reality, bolstering your travel experience with these things may seem like they're keeping you *from* your travels, but actually they're *enhancing* them. Asking real questions opens us up to real stories and invites us to learn about a place's true history. Being mindful of how you are interacting with locals puts you in a better position to get to know them as people rather than as temporary characters in your travel story. It creates a richer look at the world than you could have anticipated before. And it ensures that the generations (and houseguests) coming after you can have a similarly meaningful experience, too.

Chapter 7

LET'S BUILD THAT TRAVEL MUSCLE

"Certainly, travel is more than the seeing of sights; it is a change that goes on, deep and permanent, in the ideas of living."

—*Mary Ritter Beard*

I KNOW WE'VE SPENT A LOT OF TIME TALKING ABOUT HOW TO become the traveler you want to be: confident in solitude, gamely leaving the comfort zone, and trying to make choices about how you travel that benefit not just you but the communities you're visiting. But a key part of becoming the traveler you want to be starts with getting to know a bit about the traveler you *already are*. Only after establishing that can you become better, wiser, and stronger as a solo traveler and as a global citizen.

So...who are you, anyway?

Imagine we're having dinner and I asked you that question. If you were most people, you'd probably raise your eyebrows.

I mean...Who am I? How can anyone even begin to answer that?

As humans, we're not stagnant. We're actively changing and evolving. If we weren't, there wouldn't be much hope for us to learn or grow. I don't want you to think about your upcoming trip as "life-changing," not because it won't be, but because your life is changing all the time. This trip is a particularly powerful moment, of course. You'll learn a lot, I know. But it doesn't mean you haven't already had moments that have shaped you into who you are today. It's important to remember that, first and foremost. It takes a little pressure off to know that you've done some variation of this before.

Of course, your first solo trip is going to feel a lot different from any other trip you've been on. You're going to be challenged more than you ever have in ways that you might not have expected. You're going to practice skills you never even realized you had, and pick up new ones, too. You're going to come out of it feeling like a new person in a lot of ways, because the lessons you learn will inevitably come home with you.

We've already discussed how building a travel mindset doesn't have to happen in great leaps, so I want to use this chapter to help work that travel muscle as you prepare for your trip. Working that muscle in advance will ease your anxiety going into your trip, making the logistics of your journey smoother, while also helping your loved ones feel more secure knowing that you're not a total beginner. It'll help you bypass some of the traditional discomforts of solo travel—like tackling your own transportation logistic, or finding ways to fill time on your own—so that you can level up and embrace some of the more unique experiences of your journey without worrying about the basic stuff. And it will also give you a chance to get to know who you are now as a traveler—what's easy for you and, most importantly, what's difficult. Having an idea of your strengths and weaknesses early on will allow you to have awareness of the things that you find challenging and work on them ahead of time, making you a stronger traveler later.

When I was in college at Wellesley, I was on the varsity crew team. I'm not sure how I even made it to varsity beyond having some previous experience with rowing in high school and the fact that the crew team wasn't very good back then. I could never come close to the sheer strength and power of many of my teammates, but I had good technique, and because of that I could match the strokes of women much taller than me. I was often used as a sub when my teammates were sick or injured, because in crew, your technique can be nearly as, if not more, important than your strength. Balance, flexibility, agility, smoothness, awareness, and rhythm are all required. If you just have brute strength, you'll literally rock the boat.

In the summers, our coaches would give us training guides that we could use to practice at home to keep up our fitness while we were away from campus. They knew that we didn't have $45,000 boats at home, let alone water to row them on (or seven other people to row with). So instead of actually rowing, we had to focus on the skills that would make us better rowers with the resources we had.

I want to prescribe for you a similar pretravel regimen, which consists of giving you smaller-scale opportunities to build your travel skills without actually sending you overseas. But just like in crew, and many other sports, solely *doing* the tasks isn't enough. You'll get the most out of this training if you have awareness about what you're doing and take time to reflect on how you're feeling throughout the process. What feels more challenging? What's easier? Why do you think that is?

Sometimes, if you find you're not good at one thing, it's even more important to repeat it so that it becomes easier, or at least so that you become more comfortable with the state of discomfort. I want you to consider that here, too. This isn't just a list to check off to become Global Solo Travel Certified™ (and before you start Googling it, no, this certification does not exist). But by attempting some of these tasks, isolating what is challenging and taking the time to build your skills, you'll put yourself in a better position to embrace the breadth of your solo travel experience, rather than struggling through the smaller stuff. You'll be able to continue building on that travel muscle that you're already honing now, setting yourself up for more fulfilling, more exciting adventures later.

MEET YOUR #1 TRAVEL COMPANION: YOUR TRAVEL JOURNAL

Much like any other sports regimen, you want to make sure you have the right tools in place before you get started. In this case, there's really only one tool you'll need to practice your travels, and it's not a passport or a plane ticket. It's a travel journal.

Your travel journal can look like just about anything. Maybe it's a composition book you pick up at the dollar store. Maybe it's leather-bound with fancy beading. It doesn't matter what it looks like, really, as long as it has blank pages (lined, grid, or totally blank—it's your preference); is big enough to hold complete thoughts (no itsy-bitsy diaries, please); and portable enough to tuck into a day bag. Personally, I love having a travel journal that can track more than one trip—it makes it easier to look back and find those important reminders or special moments, but if you just want something to get yourself through the pretravel regimen, that's fine, too.

A Note on Digital Travel Journals

You may find a digital travel journal (e.g., your computer, a tablet, or even the Notes app on your phone) to be more in line with your writing style. My preference for you is a written journal—you can take it into a busy restaurant without having to pull out a laptop, you don't have to worry about battery life or weather, and it allows you to stay aware of your surroundings without being fully plugged in. That being said, the goal is to get you writing, and if you find that a digital companion—or even an audio journal—is a better extension of your voice, do what suits you best.

Your journal, however, is *not*, nor should it be, a blog. Blogs are written for other people to read. This journal should be your safe space to write what's inside your mind without worrying about if it's coming out correctly. You may use notes from your journal to support a blog later, but the texts should be different, because the audience is different.

Think of your travel journal as your best friend. I know it's mine. It will be your one lasting companion throughout your travels. The company that you'll give yourself. You'll find comfort in the familiarity of writing in your journal when everything else feels foreign—and you'll be amazed to thumb through it in the future and realize how much of your perspective on life has evolved and changed. If anything, it'll be the thing that keeps you occupied while you're alone, yet present in the moment. If you've ever been worried about what you'll do with your time when solo, or that you're going to spend a lot of moments just "staring off into space," this is the antidote. At whatever moment you feel out of place, just find the nearest table, pull out your journal, and write.

Ultimately, your travel journal will be your most prized souvenir from your trip—a capsule of not just what you did, but all the things you were thinking and feeling along this journey, the lessons you learned, and the memories you made, as well as a gift to yourself that you will be able to reopen and relive again and again.

YOUR PRETRAVEL REGIMEN

Now, let's put that travel journal to good use, shall we?

Your pretravel regimen consists of three activities that will give you the opportunity to experience all the components of solo travel, and get familiar with them, before adding in some of the logistical and cultural complexities of traveling much farther, and especially overseas. Your mission, should you choose to accept it, is to:

#1: Eat alone in a restaurant.
#2: Spend a day exploring a place solo.
#3: Book a weekend trip by yourself.

They're written in order for a reason: You should do them in that order because they build on one another. And, of course, you should write in your travel journal the whole time, observing how you think and feel, what you're finding easy and challenging, and what you're learning about yourself as a traveler in the process.

Pretravel Activity #1: Eat Alone in a Restaurant

Have you ever heard of solomangarephobia? If you know a little Latin (or perhaps you read the title of this section, you smartie, you), you may have already deduced that it refers to a fear of eating alone. Does it tell you something about how common it is that we have a specific word for it?

Even some of the most experienced solo travelers absolutely hate dining solo. We feel self-conscious being seated by ourselves. We worry that people think we don't have any friends or that we got stood up on a date. Maybe we have experience in the service industry and feel the shame of taking up a whole table by ourselves when a group of four spendthrift diners could have been seated in our place. Maybe we think we'll get the worst seat in the house, or will be hit on by the bartender or another patron, or at least constantly asked if someone is joining us. Maybe it feels awkward not knowing where to look or how to occupy our time. Maybe we just hate the idea of being bored. How will we possibly spend an hour (or longer) just... sitting there?

And, look, I get it! It's nerve-racking to show up somewhere with no idea how to get a table; the protocols around paying, tipping, or how to get the waiter's attention; and an hour (or more) of feeling like the spotlight is on us, highlighting just how alone we are (as though that's a bad thing). That anxiety is real and completely valid.

You may disagree, but I also believe that this particular concern is more elevated for women. Anecdotally, I've seen a handful of men eating in restaurants by themselves, but for women it seems rarer. Perhaps it's because we've been socialized to stay in the company of groups—a nod to the days when we, the weaker sex, needed to be escorted from place to place. Maybe a small remnant of that is still around, creating a culture where women still congregate in circles, bring friends to the bathroom, and are discouraged from simply enjoying our solitude. Whatever the case, sitting down in a restaurant and taking a moment to enjoy a bite simply because you're hungry, not being disturbed by outside forces or feeling the need to entertain yourself with banter, finding comfort in the simple company of yourself—there's an amazing amount of power in that.

I'm not talking about sitting in a coffee shop or a quick eatery (though if you've never done that, perhaps it's a good place to start). I'm talking about a restaurant with sit-down service. You might start with a restaurant you know and feel comfortable in, but at a certain point I want you to sit in a restaurant you've never been to before. Make a reservation or just stop by. If you feel particularly nervous, get an early or late seating, when the place is less busy and you won't feel too out of sorts. Bring your journal with you for a little company. Keep your phone stowed away to limit your distractions. If you're desperate for something more, try a book or magazine. That will give you something to do while keeping you from becoming too engrossed in digital media. The goal is to be mindful and present in this experience, to notice the discomfort, to embrace it, and to observe yourself.

Once you're settled at the table and have placed your drink order (and maybe requested an appetizer?), pull out your journal for a little check-in. Take a deep breath and look around you. What do you see? What's the place like? Describe it. How is your server? What did you order and why? Most importantly: How do you feel?

Take the time to listen to your thoughts and examine your mindset. Do you feel anxious or uneasy? Why? Do you feel calm? Why? Sitting in this restaurant by yourself, you're in the comfort of your native culture and language. What will it feel like for you when it's not that way? What worries you about your travels ahead? What's surprised you so far about this experience, now?

Throughout your meal, take brief moments to check in with yourself and your journal, but also make sure you're giving yourself time to be fully present where you are. Get up and take a little walk around the restaurant; look at the art along the walls (leave a scarf or a jacket at your table so your server knows you'll be right back). Actually read through the whole menu rather than rushing through it like you usually do when in the company of others. Be aware of yourself and your needs. How did you interact with your server? Were you shy? Overly loud? Indecisive? Do you have any dietary restrictions or intolerances that you'll need to communicate in the future? Make note of that, so you can be prepared for your trip with cards written in the local language explaining your dietary needs (while many servers especially in touristy or more populous areas speak English nowadays, you should never count on it, especially when it comes to your health).

Before you leave the restaurant, reflect on your overall experience. What did you spend your time thinking about while you ate by yourself? What would you like to do differently the next time you dine alone? What little nuggets, or bits of advice, do you want to leave for the "future you"?

Here's what I hope happens after your restaurant experience. I hope you feel that warm feeling in your belly. It might be from the meal (or the wine). It might also be from the satisfaction that you accomplished a small goal. Maybe you realize that it wasn't so bad after all. That it was actually kind of nice. Maybe you still feel anxious about it—and that's okay! Try again next week. Do it as many times as you need to. Don't shy away from it. The object is to have a few experiences under your belt so that dining alone feels less fraught over time, and (at a bare minimum) you know you've survived it in the past.

Finding satisfaction in eating alone is the first step to finding satisfaction in a larger solo trip. For many, it's the hardest hurdle—the time you are facing your solitude most directly, with little buffer. And in that moment of solitude when all you have to face is yourself, I hope you find a friend. If you can eat by yourself, really savor a quiet meal in your own company, and learn to enjoy that moment to check in with your feelings and your needs, you can do just about anything alone. The key is staying centered and aware. The rest is a piece of cake (which hopefully also is exactly what you had for dessert).

Pretravel Activity #2: Spend a Day Exploring a Place Solo

Who said you need two people to go on a date? Today we're going to explore the absolute pleasure of spending a day completely solo. Think about it as going on a daylong date with someone you really like. Except that person you really like is yourself.

You don't need to go far to do this one; in fact, I encourage you to stay right in your hometown or maybe the next town over. The idea is to challenge yourself to do a few things that you might not typically do on your own and spend an entire day in your own company. And yes, I do mean the *entire* day. Not just an afternoon or the whole day "but then you meet up with friends for a nightcap." Challenge yourself.

Here's what that might look like:

- Start the day off by grabbing a cup of coffee and a muffin from your favorite coffee shop. Have a seat and people-watch.
- Take a walk in one of your favorite neighborhoods. Go window-shopping. Try on hats, shuffle through some old records, or visit an antiques market.
- Treat yourself to lunch. Grab a sandwich or other travel-friendly food from a local eatery. Take it to the park for a picnic.
- Spend the afternoon visiting an art museum and gazing at the paintings.
- Go out for a nice dinner. Order a second cocktail or a fancy dessert, just because. Maybe it's one that you'd normally share with someone else, but in this case you eat the whole thing.
- Hit up a jazz bar or a show.

Sounds like a nice day, right? There are endless variations, of course. Maybe instead of the museum, you take yourself paddleboating and out for ice cream. Or you rent a bike and ride it to a farmers market and go to drag queen bingo, or you sit in for a lecture at the local university, or you get a ticket to a violin concert, or you go to the beach.

Whatever your perfect day is, make a plan, set aside a little budget, and treat yourself. Resist the urge to invite anyone along. Take your travel journal with you and find moments during your day to write about how you feel and what thoughts cross your mind. Take it out at least three times—at the beginning of your day, toward the middle, and at the end.

It might feel a little weird to spend the whole day by yourself doing things that you typically do in the company of others. It's okay to feel awkward at first. You might even feel awkward the entire time. The point is to continue to be aware of those feelings and to welcome them all the same.

Spending a day on your own also starts to work another part of your travel muscle: those logistics skills that you'll need to refine as you prepare for your solo journey. Give yourself the opportunity to really plan this day like it's a trip. Build yourself an itinerary and a budget. Then put them to work. How did you feel about the number of activities you set up for yourself? Did you plan too much and feel like you were rushing? Did you leave room for spontaneity and to enjoy the moment? How easy was it for you to navigate from one place to the next, and how much did you think about transit when you were planning? Did you keep to your budget, or did you splurge (or did you overestimate)?

This may seem like a lot of questions, but each of them holds a little bit of information that you'll be able to use for the "future you" who's planning that solo journey. The more you know how you act in new scenarios, the more you'll be able to adequately plan for your adventures ahead.

Pretravel Activity #3: Book a Weekend Trip by Yourself

Here it is! Going on a weekend getaway will be about as close as you'll get to what you'll experience on your solo trip. By which

I mean, *Surprise! You're about to go on a solo trip!* This is the sneaky moment in your couch-to-5K plan where you're running a 5K every day but it's not "the race" yet. Don't sell yourself short: This counts, too! By now, you pretty much know all the components. You're experienced with eating by yourself *and* at keeping yourself company for a day. Now you're just adding in an overnight.

Just like #2, you don't have to go far, but this time let's go beyond your hometown. Maybe just an hour or two's drive, train ride, or bus ride—far enough that you feel away from the familiar, but close enough that you have the security of home within reach if you need it. Taking a weekend (one night, or maybe two) for yourself should be a good chance to go deeper into travel planning mode and practice some of the technical components of solo travel: figuring out how you'll get there (Will you drive? Take a train? Bus?); arranging for lodging (hostel? hotel? Airbnb?); setting up child or pet care, communicating with any loved ones, and deciding exactly how you'll occupy two days of time.

I encourage you to use this opportunity to do the *hard* stuff, not the easy stuff. This isn't supposed to center on your being comfortable. This is about trying things that you might be anxious about trying abroad, but that you can do in the relative convenience of your home turf. Ever wonder what a hostel is actually like? Now's the time to try it. Glued to your car, but know you won't take it with you on your trip? Hop on a bus or train. Think you're going to carry fifty pounds of luggage with you through the streets of New Delhi? Overpack so you can get a feel for whether that's manageable. Your goal is to get as close to your upcoming travel experience as possible and to make as many mistakes as you can while in your home language, culture, currency, and time zone.

Treat your weekend away as you would the "real" trip. Visit the tourism office and get a map. Sign up for a food or walking tour. Do a little research ahead of time on the attractions that you want to visit. Make reservations at a restaurant or two. Take your dog to the kennel, or do a test run with your pet sitter. Create a document telling a loved one where you'll be staying and how to contact you in case of emergency. Make copies of other relevant documents like your hotel confirmation and your passport. Stick them in a folder. You don't actually have to give it to an emergency contact now, but going through the motions will help set you at ease for when you do it again later.

The great thing about this weekend is that you're not only in your home country, you're ideally just a few hours away from home itself. Worse comes to worst, you can always bail and go home. You don't have to worry about booking a return flight prematurely or sending your house sitter home. You can just leave.

As with the previous experiences, document everything in your travel journal. Not just what you do, but how you feel along the way:

- What parts of planning this trip were more difficult than you expected? What did you learn from those parts?
- What cool tricks and shortcuts did you learn?
- What was the best part of the trip and why?
- What do you hope you'll remember for future solo trips?
- What were you most apprehensive about? How'd it go?
- What have you learned about yourself as a traveler in this process?

The things you learn about yourself during this trip can be essential for your solo travels later. Did you love sitting quietly, gazing at that mountain range? Maybe your solo trip should include more nature, less formal planning, and more moments of unplanned time. Did you find that you got bored easily? Maybe you want to have a pretty extensive checklist so you can keep yourself occupied. Did you notice that you were getting lost all the time? Probably a good idea to get a solid footing in Google Maps, make sure you have a strong data plan on your trip, and start the practice of taking pictures of reference points so you can find your way home later.

Workouts aren't easy. That's the point. They test how well you know processes, how well you know yourself, and how well you know your limits. In the end, they make you stronger—but not without a little sweat first. Being able to explore the type of trip that you might want to take and to get acquainted with the person you'll meet while there before you actually depart is an essential way to start practicing a solo experience so you're able to make the absolute most of it. Documenting these experiences along the way in a journal will help you to reflect more deeply, plan more knowledgeably for the future, and give you a precious gift to look back on, too.

Remember: Travel is not about how many miles you go, or how many passport stamps you acquire. It's about how much you challenge yourself, how much you open yourself up to new experiences, and how much you let yourself rethink the way you look at the world.

Now, let's travel a little bit farther, shall we?

Part Three

GET OUT THERE AND EXPLORE

Chapter 8

STEP ONE: BOOK THE FLIGHT

"Diving is a leap of faith plus gravity."

—Gabrielle Zevin

A COUPLE OF YEARS AGO I SPOKE AT A LEADERSHIP CONFER-
ence for women in the military. As a military spouse myself,
I had the privilege of bringing together a panel of truly Wanderful women who were veterans and also experienced solo travelers. We were talking with an audience of women in the Air
Force about how to travel solo, whether taking advantage of solo
travel opportunities while traveling in the military or doing your
own leisure stuff. These were women who were well-traveled by
definition—their many training programs and deployments had
taken them all around the globe. When I asked the audience
members to raise their hands if they joined the Air Force because
they wanted to see the world, the room filled with hands. When
I asked them to keep their hands up if they felt they were getting

the amount of travel they were hoping for, the hands stayed up. I was pretty impressed. Okay, Air Force.

When I got off the stage, however, I was overwhelmed with personal questions. I realized that while these women may have traveled in their units many times before, they'd never actually gone into the world *alone*. The first woman approached me, her dark blond hair wrapped tightly in a bun as per military regulations. She told me a story that she had clearly been bottling up for the entire session about how her dream is to take to the road by herself. "But how do you do it?" she asked me eagerly. "How do you actually convince yourself to just *go*?"

Believe it or not, this is one of the most common questions I get about traveling alone. We can plan, dream, and talk about our solo adventures until we're blue in the face. We can understand what kind of traveler we want to be and have all our itineraries written up step-by-step in our travel journals. But at the end of the day, it's still hard to pull the trigger. That's perfectly normal. It's also why I want you to just do it. Go ahead. Book that flight right now. I'll wait...

I know that going from talking abstractly about the ways we should travel to hopping on Google Flights and dropping a few Franklins in one step may seem impulsive, but if I've learned one thing, it's that when you're thinking about doing something daring, there are a million ways you might talk yourself out of it—and if you give yourself *too much* time to ponder, the likelihood that you'll actually make a move will dwindle. That's why my top recommendation to get started on this adventure is to go all in and book the flight. Yup. Easy as that.

It doesn't mean you have to travel tomorrow. Or next week. Or even next month. It might not be until six months from now, or next year. But booking the flight allows you to make the mental leap from "I could do this" to "I'm *actually* doing this." And that will change everything. It will change how you make decisions, whom you connect with, and what resources you tap into. It will change how you look at yourself and your choices of how to spend your time between now and when you get on the plane.

By Land, Sea, or Air

You may be thinking about that first-time solo trip as an exciting, intercontinental, overseas adventure. But now you know that your trips don't have to look any certain way. Your methods of travel don't have to, either. We're going to talk about flights a lot in this chapter as that's often what springs to mind when we think about going on a solo trip, but you may also choose to drive, or take a train, bus, boat, or other method of transit. The point is not how you're traveling—it's making a commitment to actually doing it. Maybe for you the thing that will make your trip concrete is buying those hiking boots or booking a hotel. Whatever it is, I want to challenge you to make that commitment to yourself.

It's scary sometimes to call yourself out on a promise that you made to yourself, even if it was an ever-so-quiet, hardly even whispered promise that you've held deep in your heart for years. It's easy to think about what we would do if we were Cheryl Strayed hiking the PCT, but it's entirely another thing to actually put ourselves in that position, knowing that now *we* will be making mistakes and learning from them. (By the way, if you haven't read *Wild* yet, pack it for your journey. You'll love it.) It takes a lot of guts, and we may not even feel that gutsy yet.

But once you've booked your flight—probably one of the gutsiest of steps—everything else will feel easier, because you will have made the biggest leap of all: asserting that you deserve this and turning your own hopes into real action.

I know this sounds kind of nuts. "But, Beth," you might say, "I haven't even really fully decided *what I'm doing*." But that's kind of the point.

TAKING THE PLUNGE

Have you heard the statistic that women apply for only jobs that they're 100 percent qualified for, while men apply for jobs that they're only 60 percent qualified for?[1] We have been told to expect perfection from ourselves our whole lives. In order to do something—anything—we must be fully ready: 100 percent ready. But 100 percent ready doesn't exist, and it'll never happen to you in travel planning or, honestly, in anything in your life. There will always be things you don't know. There will always be a component of "figuring it out." If you plan too far in advance, you might feel like you have lots of time to work out the kinks, but you also might find that your destination has changed when you get there—for example, that a restaurant you were planning to visit has closed, or the hours of that monument you've been keen to see have changed for the season. The longer you wait, the more complexities will layer in and the more you'll question yourself—the flight logistics, the price, or the simple fact that you really *haven't* mentally committed to it yet, and this may become something you just continue to put off indefinitely.

The more we put off our travel plans, the more we can fall back into our armchair travel daydreams while watching the romanticism of a travel movie or TV show or reading a memoir. Watching bits of media that are meticulously designed and edited and perfected (and even when they're not perfect—when Bear Grylls is running away from a lion or Andrew Zimmern eats something he actually *doesn't* like—has that happened yet?—we can enjoy them from a safe, comfortable distance in our own homes). And the more we fall back into those perfect armchair travel dreams, the less likely we are to ever get out there to experience the world for ourselves.

Abandon perfect. Perfect can stay home. Perfect doesn't need to be packed into your suitcase. Perfect is going to take up too much space in your day pack. Leave her behind. Perfect is the enemy of good. Don't wait until you're 100 percent ready to book this. Aim for 60 percent. Actually, aim for 51 percent.

Yes, you read that right: If you want to make this solo trip happen, I want you to book your trip when you are 51 percent ready.

That level of ready means you have done the emotional work. You have thought about *where* you want to go and roughly how much you can spend. You've done enough work to your calendar to figure out *when* you can leave and *how long* you can be gone. But everything else is still yet to be sorted. You have no idea where you'll stay, what you'll eat, or what you'll do. You don't need any of that to book a flight. You just need to hit that 1 percent tipping point. The

1 percent that takes you from "I *could* do this" to "I *can* do this." There's a lot resting in that 1 percent. You're still going to feel 49 percent unsure of yourself; 49 percent of you is going to say, *[Your name], this is a really terrible idea.* But that part of you is outvoted now.

There are numerous studies showing that one of our biggest regrets is not traveling enough. A study by Priceline found that 44 percent of Americans regret not going on more trips.[2] Another study by Karl Pillemer, a professor of human development at Cornell University, of twelve hundred people over the age of sixty-five found that seniors often regretted not traveling more while they were young.[3] You're not going to look back on your life with regret. You're doing this.

The purpose of this chapter is to help you get to that 51 percent stage. We've talked about letting yourself be comfortable with that ongoing state of discomfort. We've talked about building the confidence to know you can do this alone. Now let's get you to the point that you feel good about two final details. After that, you'll be ready to book that flight.

- Detail #1: When am I traveling and for how long?
- Detail #2: Where am I going? (the big question)

Everything else pretty much fits into these two questions.

DETAIL #1: WHEN ARE YOU TRAVELING?

I know, I know. Everyone wants to tackle the biggest question—WHERE?—first. Of course you do. Why wouldn't you? Most of the time, the travel content you're drooling over online and in magazines is about the destination. Maybe it's a list, something like the top hidden gems around the world, or the best places to go for a safari, or (my least favorite list, but still very popular) the top safest countries for women.

I understand. We all want a little help figuring out *where* we're going, because we feel like that is the most exciting part and will give us the clearest answers about our travel plans.

But with a world full of choices, thinking about *when* and *for how long* can actually help you get an answer to the *where* question faster.

Working around a summer vacation? If you want to experience warm weather where you're going, you might want to rule out a trip to Buenos Aires, Argentina, or Auckland, New Zealand, because it's winter there. Planning a trip around a winter holiday break? Buenos Aires and Auckland might be back on the table.

If you know you can be gone for only four days, you probably don't want to travel somewhere particularly far away or with multiple layovers or big shifts in time zones. You might center your destination search on places you can travel to in four hours or less or that are direct flights only.

Think about your own parameters of travel—your number of vacation days, the time of year you can go—not as limitations, but as opportunities to focus. Restrictions can be a great way to help you narrow down your options to select the right trip for you. Most of us are planning this trip in harmony with our real lives. We're balancing jobs, housing, life events, and responsibilities (everything from your best friend's retirement party to childcare concerns). Getting clear with yourself about timing will make it that much easier to choose a destination that suits your needs and capacity in the moment.

And yes, I did say *your* needs and *your* capacity. Your first trip (I mean, honestly, all your solo trips, but the first one most especially) is about one person: YOU! While lists and social media and TV shows are great ways to pique your curiosity, they're not the be-all and end-all to travel planning. Your solo trip can happen whenever, and wherever, you want. Don't feel the need to conform to what someone has told you a solo trip should look or feel like. Everyone has different expectations, different needs, and different desires. Listen to that inner voice for yours.

Speaking of your desires, let's also set the record straight about one more thing. You may have that one perfect trip in mind. That bucket list hike in Nepal. That safari in Tanzania. But you also might find, during this process, that the timing, or budget, or some other important detail simply doesn't work. That's okay. That ideal trip you've been dreaming about doesn't have to happen right away. It doesn't have to be your first, second, or even fifth trip. Don't deny yourself the other adventures you could have just because they're not *the one* (besides, all the airline miles, travel skills, and credit card points you accumulate along the way just might make it a reality for you a little faster). In fact, I've heard stories of people waiting their whole lives for one trip, only to find that they wished they'd had a little bit more travel experience when they actually went on it. This is the beginning of what I hope will be many amazing solo travel adventures for you and many opportunities to build experience. The more experience you have, the richer each following trip will be, because your travel muscles will grow. That first trip won't be perfect (and neither will that bucket list trip). As long as you take your travel mindset with you, your travels are real and valid, whether your destination is Casablanca or Charlotte. Don't kill yourself over the pressure of that perfect destination. That level of perfect doesn't exist.

When Should I Go?

If you don't have a time in mind already, ask yourself these questions to help narrow it down:

- **What's your employment situation?** Are you taking PTO (paid time off) for this trip? What vacation time do you have, and what's already accounted for by holidays or family time? What vacation days can you merge with federal holidays to maximize your time off? Can you work remotely? Alternatively, are you planning to leave your job for a longer journey, or do you intend to capitalize on a break between jobs to travel?
- **What's your budget?** You don't need to figure out *all* the details yet, not in the least. But you probably have some general vision in your head of what you want this trip to be like. Is it a luxurious retreat somewhere warm and balmy? Is it an outdoorsy trek through the woods or the rainforest? Is it a trip to a city with a stay in a moderate hotel? Each of those comes with a different general price tag, which might help set the tone for how long you'd plan to stay and how long you'd need to save up.
- **What does your personal schedule look like?** Are there upcoming events in your life that you just can't miss (your niece's birth, the start of the school year, the enormous Eid celebration your son hosts every year, an upcoming medical procedure)? If so, when are those happening? What events are you okay with missing, if any? Leaning into your calendar and literally looking at your upcoming availability can help turn this trip possibility into a real, tangible event.
- **What do you want the weather to be like?** Knowing if you're

> wanting beachy warmth or cozy skiing weather can help you determine not just what time of year you may need to travel, but where in the world you can actually go to experience such weather during that time.
>
> - **Are you aligning with a program?** Whether it's study abroad, or a work or volunteer abroad opportunity, knowing the program dates and options might be the central focus of when you're venturing out.

The answer to length and timing will be different for each of us. If it were me planning my first solo trip all over again, I'd probably plan a week in an international destination roughly six to nine months from now. That would give me enough time to work through my pretravel regimen and take some mini trips leading up to the main trip, while also keeping my trip close enough around the corner that my life doesn't change too much in the meantime. It would also allow me to keep my job and factor in my vacation time. You may find that way too long, or too short, depending on your own hopes for yourself. Whatever you decide is okay. The key is to actually get out there and book it.

DETAIL #2: WHERE ARE YOU GOING?

So, Wander Woman, here's the Big Question: Where are you going? What's the life-changing, soul-nourishing, endlessly amazing adventure that you're about to embark on?

There are infinite ways to slice this question, and most importantly (though perhaps frustratingly), there's no wrong answer, either. In fact, it might be the one thing that's slowing you down the most. There is so much pressure to pick the right destination—the one that will change your life, right?—it can become pretty overwhelming. We end up not booking anything at all, or perpetually putting that trip off until we get busy with something else and forget about it entirely.

This book is about achieving your travel dreams, but it's also about recognizing the stroke of realism that is necessary to turn those dreams into real experiences and memories. We're turning those expectations we had of ourselves on their heads. We're turning those expectations we had of our *trips* inside out. We're finding soul-enriching experiences down the street. We're discovering places we thought we already knew. We're embracing the fact that travel will present surprises and that those surprises are some of the few beautiful things we still can't anticipate or forecast in this world. We are so loaded with technology that tells us when to purchase flights and what the weather will be and if we have any friends nearby, we forget that part of the real magic of travel—some of the true richness of it—lies simply in its serendipity. The thrill of not having any idea of what will come next.

How to Decide Where to Go

- **Sync with your availability.** This is why looking at *when* you can travel can help you decide *where*. Hopefully now you already have a sense of how long you can travel, which will give you good indicators of how far you can travel. Have only four days? You'll probably want to stay local or at least domestic. Want to go abroad for a month? You have a bit more flexibility to go far or pick a couple of destinations at once.
- **Coordinate around an event or experience.** Do you know

what month you're traveling? If so, finding special cultural events that happen in a destination you've been eyeing can be a really great way to sync your availability and the selection of a travel destination. For example, if you're free in March and India is on your list, this might be the perfect time to travel to experience a major cultural festival like Holi. Or if you have a few days in early October, that is when Albuquerque, New Mexico, hosts its International Balloon Fiesta, the largest hot air ballooning festival on earth. You might plan your trip around a concert, a favorite speaker, or a conference. Sure, every place in the world might be on your list—but events can be a really great way to justify why you should travel to a certain place *now*.

- **Choose your level of logistics.** This is your first solo trip, after all. Maybe you want to visit a place that's a bit easier on the logistics since you know you'll be going it alone. That might mean picking a place where you know the language or visiting a place with more tourism activity because you know you'll be close to a lot of English speakers. Maybe you pick a city because you don't drive and don't want to figure out transport, or a place that's only one or two hops from your time zone so that you're not dealing with too much jet lag. Maybe you take a cruise. You don't need to jump into the deep end to step outside your comfort zone. Be patient with yourself. You can always work up to other more complex travels later.

- **Get a good deal.** One of my favorite ways to travel to a new place is to literally open a flight tool like Kayak Explore or Skyscanner, narrow my travels into a general month (or a specific week), and then search "everywhere" or "all destinations." Next I'll pick a place depending on what's in my budget. Flight prices change regularly, and deals can come up. Following Travelzoo or Hopper can be another good way to catch deals when they come out. Email lists like Going (formerly Scott's Cheap Flights), Matt's Flights, and TravelPirates send flight deals right to your in-box, but act fast because they usually disappear just as quickly as they arrive.

- **Dive into your heritage or cultural curiosity.** If you have any knowledge of your family history, planning a solo trip to a destination of ancestry can be a really amazing travel experience and a way to add a level of depth to your travels. If you're not sure where you're from, you could pair it with a take-at-home DNA or ancestry test. Or pick a culture that you're simply curious about or studied in school. Have you always wanted to see the *Mona Lisa* in person? Or walk along the Great Wall of China after seeing it on the Discovery Channel? All you need is one reason to go somewhere. If something's been standing out to you in particular lately, follow that curiosity. You may have no idea what else to do when you get to China. But you'll have time to figure it out.

Of course, this is just my advice. If you're still stalling out, I'd like you to meet Pauline Frommer, copresident of FrommerMedia and editorial director of Frommer's Guidebooks. If you're thinking about the Frommer's travel guide sitting on your bookshelf right now—yup, it's that Frommer. Since 1957, Frommer's has published over 350 guidebooks and sold over 75 million copies. The thing I love about Pauline is that she is a true lover of travel for what it is: an opportunity to meet others, to embrace the unexpected, and to interact with the world. "Don't be scared of getting lost," she said to me with a smile. "You always find the most wonderful things when you get lost."

So, how would Pauline tell you to pick a destination? Her first suggestion is to focus on your budget. "I think that most travelers are looking for value," she explained. "Skyscanner gives you the ability to put in your home airport and then the word 'anywhere.' And then you can put the flights cheapest to most expensive. That's the first way to look at what might be cheapest. But you must then look at the other elements of the vacation. For a long time, getting to Iceland was the cheapest place you could go internationally from the East Coast. But once you get to Iceland, you're paying $25 for a sandwich and $200 a night for your hotel room. So it can't just be the airfare; otherwise, you could get stuck somewhere more expensive."

Pauline's second piece of advice focuses on starting really specific and broadening your scope from there. "The most rewarding vacations are ones with a purpose," she explained. "Maybe you've been a devoted bridge player all your life. And so you're going to a place where you might get to play bridge with locals." Centering your trip on something that you naturally love—then broadening your plans from there—can be a great way to help pick the right destination for you.

"I've never had a bad trip," Pauline said. "Whenever I've traveled, it's your mindset. If you go in to learn things about the local place, you're always going to find things that are intriguing. That's just the nature of travel." At the end of the day, it's about how you interpret your trip and what you learn, not necessarily about where you go. There are things to learn in every place. Having that perspective—that mindset—means the feelings of adventure and discovery will follow you everywhere.

DON'T SWEAT THE DETAILS

There are a lot of variables that may go into picking your destination and booking your flight, but here's one piece of advice that will trump all of them: Don't let yourself get caught up in the details. Not everything will fit together perfectly, and that's okay. You may have to look at your calendar a couple of times to decide when you're actually free. Or maybe you'll choose the perfect departure date and then your best friend (or your daughter) announces she's going to have a baby and it throws everything out of whack. It's okay to go back to the drawing board a couple of times; just remember that you are also making a commitment to yourself. Your family and friends are important, but so are *you*.

That's one thing that does make solo travel harder in some respects: There is no one else traveling with you, so this trip needs to become your priority and your nonnegotiable. If you come across a wall of complications (whether through scheduling, logistics, or other concerns), it's up to you to continue to be steadfast and to assert that you need this. Booking the flight ahead of time can help with that, as it can give you a justifiable fallback ("Sorry, I already booked the flight!"). At the end of the day, only you can tell yourself that you deserve to take this trip. This is that moment of self-care. This is that moment of self-connection. And by taking this trip, you are honoring the commitment you made to yourself that your experiences and your priorities matter.

There is one other thing that may set you back from getting your trip figured out, and that's the search for perfection. I've said it before, but it bears repeating: This trip will not be perfect. Yes, I know. You think you can optimize, but I promise you that a desire for perfection will only prevent you from ever getting off the ground. *Especially* if this is your first solo trip, it can feel like the pressure is on. Whether to prove to yourself or to the folks back home that you can do it, you will want this trip to go off without a hitch, and to be as dreamy, idyllic, and easy as possible. But think about it for a minute—I mean, was your first *anything* actually perfect? Your first kiss? Your first time driving a car? Your first time ice-skating? Your first day of elementary school, or high school, or university?

You may look back on your firsts with fond memories, but trust me, a lot of them weren't even remotely close to perfect, no matter how you may remember them. You probably spent a lot of time stressing over that first day of school. Maybe you brought the wrong thing for lunch because you didn't know how to pack a lunch yet. Or you didn't have the notebooks you needed, or you had *too many* notebooks. Or you wore a really cute sweater, but it was humid and warm outside. Or you forgot everybody's name. There's a reason why in the startup world we often call that first iteration of a business the "first pancake." The first pancake is never the best one. It's usually too soft or not fluffy enough for some reason. It turns out the frying pan just needed a little more time to heat up or to cool down. But that first pancake is important because it sets the stage for all the delicious pancakes after that. We don't expect our first pancakes to be perfect. Nor do we expect our first time driving a car to go smoothly. So why do we expect our first solo trip to be completely flawless?

The world really is beautiful, but it's not *only* beautiful. It's also challenging and frustrating and annoying and sometimes even ugly. Sometimes it's confusing, or at least we as travelers are confused while traveling in it. We show up at a Japanese supermarket and we buy salt instead of sugar and now those pancakes are salty. Or we check the weather meticulously before our trip and expect clear skies and beachy temperatures only to be surprised by pouring rain for two weeks straight and absolutely nothing but cute sundresses in our suitcase. Ugh!

When these things happen, we have two choices. We can get upset about it. We can decide that our day is ruined. Or we can laugh at ourselves. We can recognize that these are the fun parts of travel. You'll start to make so many of them that you'll look forward to those idiosyncratic moments that remind you you're human and you're alive. You'll take them in stride, and you'll forgive yourself. You'll give yourself room to make mistakes, to learn and grow. You'll end up buying a really snazzy jacket that you'll get compliments on for years and be able to tell an awesome story about. Maybe at some point you'll take some of those lessons home with you and be a little more graceful with yourself outside of your travels, too.

Remember how we talked about how travel is a muscle and you'll get better at it the more you exercise it? Booking that flight is your first major lift. It might feel like booking the flight is the *last* thing to do, but it's actually the *first*. It'll give you permission to start failing forward. You'll take one giant leap and the others will feel smaller. Maybe you'll spend $30 more than you intended because you're arriving on Monday instead of Wednesday. Maybe you'll realize your trip should have been eight days instead of seven. Maybe you'll make a hundred mistakes along the way. But you'll look back on this experience with fond memories—and learn a whole bunch of lessons to make you even better for the next round.

Chapter 9

IT'S TRAVEL PLANNING TIME

"Tell me, what is it you plan to do with your one wild and precious life?"

—Mary Oliver

LET'S SET THE RECORD STRAIGHT ON ONE THING: YOU'RE NOT going to build your entire travel itinerary with this book.

Trust me, not only do you not need me for that, but there are thousands—yes, literally *thousands*—of great resources that will help you plan your trip, from e-books to blogs, entire You-Tube channels, checklists, and so much more.

I won't tell you exactly how to organize your day and exactly what activities to do, because a lot of these things are personal and specific. *You* hold the reins to the trip you want to take. In fact, my hope is that one day you can show up in a new place with no plan whatsoever and feel totally cool as a cucumber. Not cool in the sense of "I've seen everything and this is boring," but cool in the sense that it's still exhilarating and new and scary but you have complete and utter confidence in yourself and know you can handle making it up as you go.

What I want to do is help add tools to your tool belt so you can get out there confidently and safely, not just on this trip but every trip hereafter. Instead of hacks and must-sees and don'ts, I want to introduce you to a framework for things you should figure out in advance, at least to a degree. This is where you should spend your planning time over the next few months (or weeks, depending on when that departure is) as you get ready for your trip. Each item takes a little bit of thought and research. You might try to sort out one at a time, but you might also equally find that they sometimes intersect with each other. You might not be able to finalize one until you're farther down the line with the other. That's okay.

Here are five areas you want to focus on while in trip planning mode:

1. Hash out your budget.
2. Decide where you'll stay.
3. Embrace under-planning.
4. Identify your strings.
5. Know your exit strategy.

HASH OUT YOUR BUDGET

Throughout this book, we've spent a fair bit of time talking about money implicitly. We walked through the financial privilege of being able to travel in the first place and the fact that sometimes the more responsible travel option is also more expensive. We discussed haggling and why you shouldn't do it (so much). You even figured out an overall budget *idea* for the type of trip you wanted to take. But there's a big difference between having the general sense of how luxurious this trip is going to be and actually breaking down your planned expenditures, and now it's time to talk turkey. So let's take a moment to figure out and maximize your budget, and talk about how to splurge smartly (yes, there is such a thing).

How to Choose a Budget

There's nothing that will ruin a trip faster than an unanticipated credit card bill or an overdraft fee. Sometimes life happens, but getting clear about your budget up front—both what you need to be prepared to spend and what you can afford to spend—will help you make the most of your trip and avoid nasty surprises.

Travel budgeting is more or less straightforward, but there are a few key differences from at-home budgeting, especially when you're traveling solo. First of all, you might have very little information about how much things *cost* in your destination. Are you traveling to Switzerland, where you might spend $8 on a cucumber, or Thailand, where you might spend $8 on a hotel room? A quick Google search can help reveal general prices of groceries and hotel rooms so you know what parameters you're working under. (By the way: Don't think there aren't ways to travel on a budget in northern Europe, of course. You're just going to have to get more creative.)

The second thing to be prepared for is the fact that it's easy for things to get a little more expensive if you don't watch your wallet. Oftentimes, the more economical choices come paired with a party of two or more—think of the double-occupancy hotel room or the pitcher of sangria at dinner. As a solo traveler, you don't benefit from buy-one-get-one-half-off tickets to a tour or museum, and you can't split the cost of cabs, a hotel, or a couple of entrées at dinner to sample more of the local cuisine. Traveling solo doesn't have to cost twice as much as traveling with a partner, but it can if you don't watch yourself.

The Single Supplement

For those of you who don't know about the dreaded single supplement, it's a fee added to planned travel like cruise lines or multiday tours where the bookings are typically made double occupancy. The supplement offsets the income that the cruise line misses when you're not booking two tickets in one cabin. But don't let that scare you. While the single supplement is very common in some areas of travel, in other spaces—like most hotels, or any type of travel where you're doing the bookings yourself—it doesn't even exist. There are other times when cruise lines will waive the single supplement fee as part of a sale. With the rise of solo travel, single supplements are also losing popularity—but they're still out there.

To make sure you don't have too many surprises, go into your trip with a basic outline of your spending expectations. It will help you make smarter decisions on the ground, especially because when you are fully enamored with your trip, it's easy to start spending more loosely. Knowing what your spending limits are in advance can help you plan for that feeling now. (*No, Beth, you do NOT need one of those pretty skirts in every color; one is enough!*)

Your travel budget is likely going to fit into some version of the categories listed below, segmented into what you've paid for before departure and what you might pay for on the ground.

Things you might pay for in advance:

- Lodging (hotel, homestay, etc.)
- Transportation (flight, bus/train fare, shuttle to your destination, etc.)
- Logistics (travel insurance, suitcase, additional gear you'll need to purchase, etc.)

Things you might pay for on the ground:

- Foods and beverages
- Local transit (taxi, subway)
- Activities (museum tickets, walking tours)
- Souvenirs

Because you're spending money on your trip at different times, I recommend you give yourself an *overall budget* (which incorporates the total you want to spend on this trip) as well as a *daily budget* (which incorporates how much you intend to spend out of pocket per day on incidentals like food and attractions). Of course, you can map out your trip any way you want, but for me, having a good grasp of these two figures is a solid way for me to plan correctly in advance and manage my wallet on the ground. Your solo weekend away (part 3 of your travel prep regimen) is a great opportunity to put that plan into action. While the economics of the place you're visiting may be different, the types of experiences you want (luxury hotel or campground? restaurant or grocery store for dinner?) may be similar, as well as your own spending patterns and values (Are you more interested in spending on experiences or lodging? Are you good at sticking to a budget or do you regularly go over it?).

Fees, Fees, Fees

Keep in mind that one thing you'll want to account for in your budgeting that you might not have at home is fees. That may include foreign transaction fees on your credit card, ATM withdrawal fees, and even conversion rates for your local currency. There are lots of great resources and creators to follow to get savvy on travel credit cards, points, and everything finance-related. The Points Guy is an industry favorite. Angel Trinh of Pennywise Traveler and Julia Menez of Geobreeze Travel are also great women creators to follow.

Budgeting = Traveling Like a Local

I often get questions from eager travelers about my top recommendations for traveling like a local. Do you know what I tell them? Stick to a budget.

Let me explain: A few years ago, I traveled to New Orleans for a wedding. Ever the budgeter, I in my financial savviness booked an Airbnb just outside of the French Quarter. It was inexpensive, clean, and the best part? It was just a ten-minute Uber ride to pretty much anywhere I needed to go downtown. On my first day in the city, I was in a major rush and pulled out my app. I was pleasantly surprised that Ubers were about $10 each way (compare that to the $20 or $30 I might have dropped for a ten-minute ride in Chicago, where I was living at the time). That sounded totally reasonable, right?

At first, a $10 Uber ride was great. But those totals added up fast. After the wedding, I Ubered to the restaurant. After the restaurant, I Ubered home. The next day, I Ubered to the park, to a friend's place, to a café. A few days in, I looked at my spending and realized I had spent well over $100 on Uber rides. How did that money disappear so fast?!

At that point, I'd had enough. I pulled open my computer and searched "New Orleans public transportation." That brought me to the Regional Transit Authority (RTA) website, where I found out that a Jazzy Pass—unlimited daily use of their streetcar and bus system—would cost me a grand total of $3.

Yup, the $150 I'd spent over the last three days could have easily been about $9 if I had just spent five minutes looking at my options and planning ahead. And not to mention, the streetcars in New Orleans are VERY cute (I ended up spending my next three days riding exclusively on them and enjoying some fantastic views).

I tell you this story because it applies to every one of us at some point, especially when we're traveling solo. We hop in a cab because we didn't take a minute to look at options or because we're operating on autopilot. We eat out every night and then realize that we were a two-minute walk from a really awesome local farmers market. We get so wrapped up in the destination we're visiting, we don't think clearly about the fact that our exciting travel experience is someone else's everyday normal. Our destination is someone else's home, and trust me, no one spends their entire day Ubering everywhere (except an Uber driver).

There are times and places for luxury travel, but even if you're not really a budgeter, some of the tactics that you use to travel on a budget are nearly identical to the tactics you'd use to travel like a local. In fact, sticking to a budget in some ways is one of the most immersive ways to travel that we have. It forces us to examine the realities of people who are locals in places rather than getting a perfectly curated visitor's view.

Good Ways to Travel on a Budget *and* Like a Local

- **Shop at the local grocery store.** Rather than eating out every day, pick up a few necessities to make a quick breakfast or pack a lunch. Besides saving you some money, little things like learning how much Brie costs in France versus in the States will blow your mind. Find the local farmers market and make a day of it talking to the vendors.
- **Take local transit.** Understand the local transit system and take that rather than taxis and rideshares everywhere, especially if it's the middle of the day. (There are no hard-and-fast rules here; if you're traveling late at night or if it's your first day in the city and you're exhausted, you're not breaking any "local travel" guidelines by taking a taxi for convenience or safety. The point here is, just don't make it your *only* option.) Explore other fun ways to get around, like using a bike or scooter rental program, hopping on a motorcycle taxi, or just walking.
- **Take advantage of free days and discounts at local attractions.** Many museums offer free days (there is a caveat to this; free days tend to be much, much busier). Popular attractions often have student and senior discounts. Some will require an international student ID card; others will accept your student ID or, for a senior discount, your passport. If you're hanging around for a while, some locations have city passes for one flat rate that give you access to

multiple top attractions. Visit your destination's local tourism office website, or stop in when you arrive and ask them.

- **Be mindful of souvenirs.** We've talked about the reason for this as it relates to waste. Being caught up in the moment, you'll find that souvenirs can easily become a slippery slope. Just one item can turn into ten or fifteen pretty quickly. (What about my boss? My coworkers? The front desk staff at my office...?) That impulse to buy will be frequent: Know it and expect it, and create boundaries ahead of time. Consider making a list in advance of those you're buying for or limiting the number of items you purchase. Intentionally bring a small suitcase so you don't have room for more. Or just take photographs and get them printed at home when you're away from the pressure to buy. If you must buy gifts, give them a dual purpose, like making them holiday or birthday gifts. But remember: At the end of the day, this solo trip is about you. Limiting your souvenir purchasing isn't being greedy. No one should be expecting anything from you. Don't let yourself be so overwhelmed thinking about what souvenir to get for whom that you miss the point of this solo trip entirely.

It's Okay to Splurge (Sometimes)

I know we're talking about budget travel and how traveling like a local can help you stay on budget, but at the end of the day, you're not a local—you're a tourist. So what's one thing that you really do want to drop a bunch of change on? A boat tour of Victoria Falls in Zimbabwe or Zambia? A full spa day in a Korean bathhouse? It's okay to splurge a little, especially on a cornerstone experience, and knowing in advance what you *do* want to spend your money on can help you intentionally de-prioritize other things. Yes, we all want to be the coolest, most flexible, down-to-earth travelers ever. But we all deserve to treat ourselves, too. The key is anticipating when and where that will happen so it doesn't overtake the entire trip.

DECIDE WHERE YOU'LL STAY

For many solo travelers, the best part of traveling alone is the simple fact that you get to make all your own choices. You're not limited by someone else's needs or desires. Want to spend an entire day looking at one painting? Amazing! Want to lie on the beach and read for five hours? Go for it! It's all up to you.

Lodging as a solo traveler is like that, too. When you're traveling alone, there are actually more unique and interesting choices on where to stay because you're not limited to so many logistical needs, like needing a crib for a baby, or a kitchen to cook for a family, or a room big enough for a couple. Things you might have never considered while traveling with a group become very reasonable options (and very inexpensive, too).

Whether you're more interested in the comfort of a trusted brand or want something a little more community-oriented or adventurous, you have a lot of options. Let's take a closer look.

The Old Standbys: Hotels, Inns, and Bed-and-Breakfasts

When it comes to safety, security, and trust, the world of traditional hospitality—hotels, inns, and bed-and-breakfasts—still tops the list of lodging options for many. For one thing, you know you're going to be taken care of (maybe even pampered). You get to benefit from a score of amenities, whether it's an on-site spa or restaurant, a fitness center, or logistical support like airport transfers. You'll have a team of experts (i.e., the hotel staff) waiting to help you out. And if you're particularly concerned about safety, nothing can beat the comfort of the Old Standbys.

Depending on where you stay, you may be loaded up on conveniences, but that doesn't mean you have to surrender a local experience. Maybe instead of staying with a familiar chain, you opt for a small locally owned bed-and-breakfast where you can connect with the owners. Maybe you intentionally find a hotel that shares a lot of your same values, whether that's being minority owned and operated or sustainable and eco-friendly. Maybe you opt for a hotel for your first night or two to help yourself settle in, but then move onto something different later on in your trip. Or maybe having that known-quality hotel as a home base gives you the confidence to take on other kinds of adventures. Where you stay doesn't have to be the defining quality of your trip, and there are ample ways to incorporate local qualities while also giving yourself the benefit of comfort. Hotels have been around for thousands of years. There's a reason for that.

The Local Hosts: Airbnb, Vacation Rentals, and Homestays

In 2007, two young guys named Brian Chesky and Joe Gebbia were broke and looking to earn some money so they could make their rent in San Francisco. They knew that hotels were booked up for a popular conference in town, so they decided to rent out air mattresses in their apartment. That concept turned into Airbnb, the behemoth vacation rental company that has completely changed the way many of us travel.

The original concept of Airbnb was to live like a local—hosts would rent out private and shared spaces in their home and make money off them. The lodging fee was a key modification to existing players like Couchsurfing, which was founded in 2004 and generally offered couches to sleep on for free. While Airbnb was different from vacation rental companies like Vrbo, which had been around since 1995 and offered entire homes and apartments for short-term rent, it's become more like it; now nearly 80 percent of Airbnb bookings are entire homes.

If you're looking for privacy and a kitchen, one-bedroom Airbnbs and studios are great for solo travelers. You can embed yourself in a neighborhood and feel like you're actually living there. Sometimes, even with a whole property to yourself, you're still geographically close to the host (I once stayed in an apartment that was next door to the owner's main family home in Athens, and his mother would bake fresh bread with honey every morning for guests—to die for). Historically, vacation rentals have been cheaper than hotels, but that has also changed in recent years. Some have high cleaning fees, are managed by vacation rental management companies, and have the look and feel of a more generic rental than someone's real home. There's a balance to strike for sure, but there are still great Airbnbs out there. Plus, they can become particularly economical and comfortable if you're staying for a longer period of time, giving you access to a kitchen and generally more private space than a hotel room.

If you're staying solo in an Airbnb or vacation rental, privacy, security, and great reviews are important to keep an eye on. I've heard horror stories of women who have checked into private rooms on Airbnb only to discover that the property had other bedrooms and those bedrooms were rented out by other guests without any host on-site, serving as a de facto hotel with no management. And of course, there are always scams, which sites like Airbnb are constantly trying to protect against (but still exist). While the sharing economy is generally safe and fun, it has its drawbacks, which is why your best bet is to read the reviews and rent under a Superhost.

Beyond Airbnb

Want to have the experience of living like a local? While Airbnb made the idea of staying in another person's home mainstream, there are a number of ways you can have an amazing homestay experience outside of Airbnb. Try:

- Community Homestay Network, based in Nepal, is a community-run program that puts travelers up in local homes as a way to benefit the local economy and has expanded throughout the entire country and paved the way for other community homestay networks around the world.
- Couchsurfing originated as free couches to crash on around the world. Now they organize meetups and other activities for travelers to connect.
- Golightly is a private women's vacation rental network founded by Victoria O'Connell after her London flat was burglarized by a group of men who booked her place on a popular homesharing site. The intent of Golightly is to create an invite-only, safer alternative for women-identifying guests to find places to stay around the world. If you don't know anyone already on the platform, you can still apply to join.
- TrustedHousesitters is a platform that you can use to stay in someone's home and take care of their pets while they're away. Besides an annual fee, the homestays are usually free.
- Wanderful's Global Hosting Network is a portion of our membership community where you can find places to stay with other members—whether a spare bedroom, a guesthouse, or something else.
- WWOOF is one of the original travel plus lodging on a budget programs, where you get free room and board in exchange for working on an organic farm.

The Community Spaces: Hostels and Hybrids

If you saw the 2005 film *Hostel*, you know it definitely didn't do a whole lot of justice to the hostel world. In the film, two backpackers looking for sex end up in a hostel of horrors, where characters are routinely maimed and tortured. The real tragedy, though, is that many Americans were not familiar with hostel life before this movie—and let's just say that movie swore them off one of the coolest ways to travel for a long, long time.

Even if you didn't see *Hostel*, hostels in general don't always have the best reputation. We often think of them as being filled with young partyers, quite loud, not particularly private (rooms filled with eight bunk beds often spring to mind), and basically a nightmare for any self-respecting adult. Are there hostels out there that are still like that? Absolutely. But are all hostels like that? Not at all. In fact, if you'll humor me for a moment, you might find that hostels are some of the best ways to travel solo on earth.

In my experience, hostels are an amazing way to have a rich travel experience at virtually any age. Many nowadays are clean, modern, and come with loads of amenities. Many have also removed their age limits, so you'll see hostel-goers in their twenties, but also some in their seventies. To appeal to a more age-diverse audience, many hostels have incorporated private room accommodations, even with en suite bathrooms. And the intent of all of them is to give you a glimpse of your destination at a fraction of the price of a hotel.

Hostels are ideal travel options for solo travelers not just because they're inexpensive, but also because they give you natural opportunities to interact with other travelers from around the world, adding a whole other nuance to your travel experience. Many have large kitchens that you can use to store and prepare food, and others have free walking tours and other social activities that help you learn about your new city from an experienced tour guide. They're often located quite close to downtown, giving you easy walking access into the major hub of the city, if not ever-so-slightly on the outskirts.

"Don't be scared of hostels," Pauline Frommer told me. "Hostels can be extraordinary, not only money savers, but a built-in social community. In that lobby, you're going to meet people; and in your room, you're going to meet people. Solo travel is really a misnomer. You're never a solo traveler. You're always meeting people."

Some hostels have been recognized for their design aesthetic, winning prestigious awards. And others, like Hostelling International, are actually nonprofits, using their earnings to fund national and international exchange programs. Many have on-site cafés or restaurants and offer free breakfast. If you do share a room with other hostel guests, make sure you check the website to know what's included. There may be lockers, so you'll want to bring a lock. You might also be asked to bring your own towel or linens, though some hostels now offer rentals for a small fee. Then again, there are other things hostels have that you'd never get in a hotel—cookware, for example, or a free library, or leftover snacks shared by other travelers. A hostel is also a great pick for your pretravel weekend by yourself, because you can get a taste of what they're like and what you should actually pack.

With the rise of remote work, coworking players like Selina who focus on a digital nomad audience have found a happy place that exists between a hotel and a hostel. These hybrids offer smaller, more spartan rooms that are more like a hotel room, but with a daily menu of community activities like workouts, game nights, live music, workspace, strong Wi-Fi, and more. If you're the kind of person who likes to be around people, but also doesn't want to sacrifice a comfortable bed with a pillowtop mattress, a hybrid might be the right choice for you. Because they often focus on people who are working while traveling, their audience can skew younger—something to keep in mind if you're looking for a little more age diversity.

The Outdoorsy Types: Camping and Glamping

No proper solo travel guide could leave out one of my favorite types of travel: exploring the outdoors. As a seasonal hiker and camper who grew up not far from the mountains in New Hampshire, I absorbed through osmosis one of the telltale rules of the outdoors: Never hike or camp by yourself. If you're alone and something happens (even something relatively small like tripping on a rock and spraining your ankle), it's a lot harder to get help or, God forbid, be found. I always cringed hearing about solo hikers getting lost and succumbing to the wilderness.

But in recent years, some great outdoor experiences have become available that allow you to embrace the spirit of the outdoors while also giving you access to company and community (when you want it), from traditional RV parks and campgrounds, to trendier glamping and Airstream resorts like AutoCamp.

Much like your hostel experience, a key part of doing this type of travel alone is paying close attention to what you'll need to pack. A traditional campground will expect you to bring everything (tent, sleeping pad or mattress, and all). This in itself might require a whole new set of skills that you don't have yet (how to build a fire, how to identify potable versus nonpotable water, etc). Joining a local camping and hiking group might be a good option to help you earn your sea legs before you go it alone (a quick Google search can help you identify what's near you, and there are also some helpful suggestions in the Resources sections of this book).

Alternatively, if just being in the outdoors is what you're looking for, a glamping retreat might be a better way to achieve this without having to learn wilderness skills. Staying in one will be more akin to an outdoor hotel. I once stayed in a luxury tent in Cape Cod that was equipped with its own French press and locally roasted coffee. These types of lodging also often have community events, like yoga classes and live music; my resort had bikes for rent, s'mores kits, and a giant chessboard on the lawn. There are also really cool deep-in-the-woods tiny houses like Getaway House, which are outfitted with heat, electricity, and a cozy firepit for those Henry David Thoreau–inspired moments of self-connection.

If this is the type of solo trip you're gunning for, you might already realize that you're going to get a lot more quality time with Traveler #1 (you) than at other types of accommodations. Your travel journal is going to get a good workout here, so make sure you bring a fresh one with lots of pages.

Thinking About an Outdoor Adventure?

The outdoors should be for everyone. Unfortunately, people of color and other marginalized groups have traditionally been excluded from outdoor travel. While there are formal programs working to change that, there are also tons of incredible communities for outdoorsy women of various intersections to check out, including:

- Brown People Camping (woman-run and open to anyone), Melanin Base Camp, and Outdoor Afro, communities focused on supporting Black and brown people in the outdoors
- Disabled Hikers
- Flash Foxy, for women climbers
- Latinxhikers
- Love Her Wild, a nonprofit women's adventure community based in the UK
- Native Women's Wilderness, a nonprofit created for Native women to celebrate the wilderness of their native lands
- LGBT Outdoors, connecting queer people with the outdoors
- She Dreams of Alpine, an outdoor adventure blog to demystify the outdoors for women
- Unlikely Hikers, which advocates for body inclusivity and anti-racism in the outdoors
- Women's RVing communities like Sisters on the Fly and Girl Camper

EMBRACE UNDER-PLANNING

I know, this one is not easy at all. If you're a planner, the idea of under-planning sounds offensive, blasphemous even. Why would I spend all my money traveling to a place only to *not* do everything I can possibly think and dream of?

When I say embrace under-planning, I'm not saying do nothing. What I'm saying is, don't try to do everything. Be thoughtful and intentional with your time. Sometimes we can get so caught up in making lists of all the things we want to see that we forget the opportunity we have to just sit with ourselves apart from any outside forces and stresses of our everyday lives. The beauty that comes when you have a free afternoon and can follow whatever whim inspires you. The ability to say yes to an unexpected opportunity or adventure.

If you're a super planner, you might consider *planning in* unplanned time. Yes, it sounds a bit antithetical. But the goal here is to make sure you're giving yourself room for spontaneity. If you're always running for your timed entrance to the next monument, how can you enjoy the cultural festival you stumble across? Have a reservation for absolutely every meal weeks in advance? You might miss out on that delicious-smelling corner spot you find on your explorations.

I also want to recognize how tiring solo travel can feel. Because you are exercising your brain (and likely your legs) pretty much all day with little relief, and because you might be doing these things without the comforts of your native language and culture, there's a good chance you'll find yourself more quickly drained than when you're traveling in a group (you also might find yourself more energized; who knows?). As you build your travel itinerary, keep that in mind. You might want to plan only one key activity per day, or schedule your planned activities for the morning or the afternoon, so that you have natural built-in free-choice time.

Here's how to thoughtfully under-plan: Take a moment to identify the "absolute musts" of your trip. What are one to three things that you feel like you absolutely *need* to do? You might find it hard to narrow it down, but you might also realize that, even though you have a long list of things you'd *like* to do, there's not one single thing that would ruin your trip if you missed it. That's fantastic! Realizing that none of those things are absolute musts doesn't mean you don't care. It just means that you're open and flexible. That even if you don't end up making time for the things you had planned, you know you are still capable of having a wonderful trip.

In an article I read about FOMO, or fear of missing out, the author suggested that we should actually *embrace* missing out, rather than fear it. Every time we miss out on something, it means that we are purposefully choosing to spend our time and energy on something else that we determine is more important. Keep that in mind as you decide on your key priorities for your trip. What's an absolute must? What will you live without if you end up opting for something else?

A Note on Choosing What's Right for You

This chapter has numerous ideas on how to optimize your trip, from picking where to stay to what to spend your money on. Remember, the key point is that this trip is for you, and you should ultimately do what is right for the type of traveler you are.

"I get irritated reading travel blogs and watching travel videos where people brag about trying all the different street food, staying in hostels to save money, traveling light (just a backpack), and always seem to be smiling and happy. That's not my experience, and yet that type of content makes me feel guilty," neurodivergent travel creator Kayley Whalen shares. "Being neurodivergent has meant that I need to be aware of my own limits and find ways to accommodate my own unique needs without feeling shame or guilt. I can't stay in hostels or group/shared living because I need a lot more alone time to recharge. I have digestive problems and can't eat the vast majority of what other people eat. I need to carry extra luggage to take care of my health and medical needs."

Ultimately, the key to planning the right trip starts with *knowing and accepting yourself*. Should you step outside your comfort zone and try everything at least once? Absolutely. Should you put pressure on yourself to do things that make you miserable just because everyone else tells you that's the "right" way to travel? No way.

IDENTIFY YOUR STRINGS

Sometimes a big hang-up I have about how we [the avid travelers] talk to people who want to travel but haven't yet is that we make travel sound like this amazing offer with no strings attached. "All you have to do is take the plunge!" we exclaim. "Step one: Book the flight!" (For those who cannot understand my own dry humor, yes, I am well aware that this is, in fact, the exact title of the last chapter.)

While some of us have the luxury of being able to close our eyes and hop on a plane whenever we want, realistically, that's not all of us (or even most of us). We have commitments or jobs. We have kids, or aging parents, or a friend who needs us. We have pets. We have rent to pay. These are the "strings" that I like to say we forget about in that "no strings attached" travel pitch, those little pieces that pop up *riiiiiight* when you're about to book your flight. There you are, cursor hovering over the "purchase" button, when you think, *Wait a minute, what am I going to do about my iguana/job/succulents/parent-teacher conference/sourdough starter/house/ongoing feud with the neighbor over parking spots while I'm gone?*

Your strings are the pressing needs in your life that will need to be addressed before you can actually depart. Of course, there's nothing wrong with having strings. We all have them. I have kids, a husband, a mortgage, a café where it seems like some piece of equipment is always breaking, two eighty-pound dogs, and a plot in my community garden. Oh, and an orchid (God forbid I forget to keep her humid). It doesn't mean that I can't travel alone. It means that I need to work out more logistics before I leave. Identifying what your strings are is a key part of making sure you give yourself the freedom to get out there. The longer you ignore them, the more they'll creep back on you later and tie you down. Your strings are the pressing needs in your life that will need to be addressed before you can actually depart.

For some people, the biggest string tethering them to home is not a responsibility or a particular relationship, but the plain and simple fact that they have concerned friends and family members who are urging them out of the trip to begin with. If you have announced your interest in traveling solo before to a loved one and been met with wide eyes and a short monologue about safety, then you might have some emotional strings to address (you may also be the type of person who ignores this concern completely, which is what I did with my moderately concerned parents, but everyone is going to have their own way of dealing with this).

What to Tell Liam Neeson (or Any Concerned Parent, Friend, or Other Loved One) about Your Solo Trip

Script ideas that go beyond "I'll be fine":

- "I have given a lot of thought to this trip, and while I understand that no one is ever 100 percent risk-free anywhere, I trust myself to make the best choices I can to keep myself safe. If you need me, know that I'll just be a phone call away."
- "My safety is of the utmost importance to myself, too. That's why I've [purchased travel medical insurance/invested in a flight with no change fees/printed an itinerary/alerted my

local embassy] and created a backup plan in case things go wrong."

- "While I love and appreciate that you are worried about me, this is a choice that I have made for myself and at this moment what I can hope for is your respect and understanding."

Let's take a moment for the fact that we women in particular often have a LOT of strings. Women are still responsible for the majority of childcare and other caregiving. Society expects us to do this in addition to our full-time jobs, if we have them. If we're full-time parents, the thought of going on a solo trip sounds almost incendiary. These pressures factor so heavily into our ability to find a time to travel, as if we can leave only when it's maximally convenient for everyone else. For some, this will be endlessly frustrating. It might feel like you can't find even a moment to step away from your responsibilities. But asserting your own self-care makes you a better caregiver, too (and might help you find long-term ways to outsource or share responsibilities with others). Don't let your strings (no matter how cute they are, or how much they love you) keep you from living your own life, too.

Being able to take the time to address your strings up front can save you a lot of headache later when trying to enjoy your travels. The other thing that will help them (and also help you) is my last tip, which is to have a clear exit strategy.

KNOW YOUR EXIT STRATEGY

No one—and I mean no one—likes to think about exit strategies, yet, as entrepreneurs, the concept is hammered into our heads from day one. Investors will look at your perfectly polished business plan and say "So, what happens if all this fails?"

or "How are *you* planning to leave the business?" At first it's really annoying. You think up your best fake answer (not dissimilar from the "What are your weaknesses?" question that you get in job interviews, where the strategy is to think up something that's not *actually* a weakness, like "I work too hard!" or "I'm too dedicated!"). You fire back with a list of businesses that will one day want to acquire yours. You talk about going public.

But the longer I've been a business owner and experienced the highs and lows of running a business, the more I understand the true nuances of having an exit strategy. Taking the time to *really* think through what will happen—when your business partner bails, when you run out of money, when you're committed to hosting a giant festival and then there's a global pandemic (okay, I don't think any of us saw that one coming, but still it happened to me)—is not just an important part of planning; it's absolutely essential. It accomplishes two key things: It gives you a path forward for when things do go awry, and it allows you the freedom to figure things out because you've already done the heavy lifting.

This isn't unlike travel, either. We don't like to think about things going wrong. And for the most part, the "going wrong" moments are small hiccups along the way. But if something *does* happen—something that you really couldn't have anticipated—knowing that you have a fallback plan is an amazing gift you give yourself.

These fallbacks might look like a few things in particular, including:

- **Creating a travel folder.** Make hard copies of important documents like your passport. Print out your itinerary and your hotel reservations. Include credit card numbers to make it easy to cancel any cards you lose or that get stolen. You might have done all of this during your pretravel regimen. Throw it into a folder (or a secure digital folder if you want to save paper) and share it with a loved one back home. This way if something happens, someone you trust will know where you are.

- **Registering with the Smart Traveler Enrollment Program (STEP).** The US Department of State offers STEP for free to US citizens. It's a website where you can register your current location when you're traveling so that the State Department can contact you in case of an emergency or a disaster at home or in your destination. It's fast, it's free, and it's a really important fail-safe that I recommend to every American traveler going abroad.

- **Arranging for medical evacuation insurance.** We often think of medical evacuation insurance, like Global Rescue or Medjet, being just for the most gutsy of all of us—that person who's climbing Mount Everest, for example. But actually these insurances are very reasonably priced and take a whole lot of weight off your shoulders. Many of them have access to an English-speaking doctor just a phone or a tap away, which can be incredibly useful if you have a food allergy or chronic illness, but also useful if you develop a weird rash after swimming somewhere, or have really bad menstrual cramps, or eat something that keeps you in the bathroom all afternoon. If you have concerned friends or family members, knowing that you have coverage to get immediate, free medical attention if you need it can be an enormous relief for them as well (this is my mom side talking, of course—but really, it'll save me many nightmares when my children are older). Basic travel medical insurance can also do the job, depending on what your needs are and where you're going.

- **Making sure you've got a credit card with some available credit and knowing who you'll call.** What if you decide during this solo trip that the best thing for you is to go home, and now? Making sure you've addressed those barriers before you leave is essential. Take time to think about who you might call in case of an emergency—a best friend, maybe, or a partner. Have their number written down somewhere so you can reach them even if you lose your phone and their number slips your mind (no matter how obvious; in moments of stress I have forgotten some of the most important and obvious phone numbers). Ensure you have a credit card with some available credit on it in case of emergency so you can buy a flight and get back home.

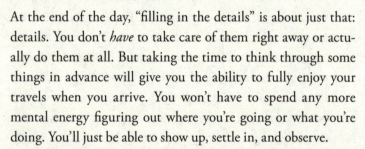

At the end of the day, "filling in the details" is about just that: details. You don't *have* to take care of them right away or actually do them at all. But taking the time to think through some things in advance will give you the ability to fully enjoy your travels when you arrive. You won't have to spend any more mental energy figuring out where you're going or what you're doing. You'll just be able to show up, settle in, and observe.

Of course, there is one thing that you *do* have to do before you arrive: You have to pack something (anything). And when you're on your own, there are a few key things you should know about ahead of time to set yourself up for success. We'll talk about that next.

Chapter 10

MOM SAYS DON'T FORGET YOUR FAKE WEDDING RING: PACKING FOR YOUR SOLO TRIP

"You are the one that possesses the keys to your being. You carry the passport to your own happiness."

—Diane Von Furstenberg

IT'S AUGUST 2006. I'M SITTING ON THE FLOOR OF MY BEDROOM. A sea of blue carpet surrounds me, but you can barely see it because it's covered in a mess of things: shirts and dresses and shoes and books and toiletries. A giant orange suitcase sits in front of me, the suitcase that is supposed to encapsulate my life for a whole year while I study abroad in Portugal. How do you even begin to pack that?

My mother knocks quietly on the door and opens it. She sits down next to me and hands me a small drawstring jewelry bag. She does this from time to time when she's going through her things and wants to give me something important, a family heirloom. It always kind of happens as an afterthought, without any major presentation. Just "Oh, I found this." But this time she's really excited about it; she wants me to open it right then and there.

I open the bag and turn it over into my palm. Out spills a silver ring with a giant diamond. It shines and glitters, and I turn it this way and that to catch the light. But after a moment, as I look deeper at its perfect clarity, I realize it's lightweight. It's not silver, and it's not a diamond at all.

"It's a fake engagement ring," she says proudly. "So now no one will hit on you."

Ah, parents. Fear and love, right?

I open with this story because, as a woman preparing for her first solo trip, you are going to get a *lot* of advice about what you need to take with you. Some of that advice will come in the form of listicles in the same vein as the "Top 10 Countries for Solo Female Travelers" articles—they'll either be a slew of safety-focused products (door stoppers, whistles, you name it) or completely irrelevant roundups related to fashion trends and how to look cute. More general, nongendered packing lists will try to convince you to pack just about everything under the sun (an emergency blanket, electrolyte drink packets, a bungee cord, a headlamp—yup, even if you're going to Paris) because these lists look better if they're longer and more comprehensive (and they perform better in search results).

Offline advice will find you, too. You don't even have to look very hard for it. Well-meaning friends and loved ones will swear by a certain product or device, and they'll let you know about it. You may even be gifted things, as if your possession of this one item is the sole key to your being safe, happy, and comfortable.

You may welcome this advice. You may scour the internet for packing lists and suggestions. That's completely okay. Travel packing can be an enormous anxiety for a solo traveler. Just as you're responsible for all your travel decisions, so you are also responsible for deciding what you need and don't need—and if you forget toothpaste, you can't just borrow someone else's; it's just you. That's a lot of weight on your shoulders, and you haven't even put on your backpack yet!

As a society, we become fixated on packing almost as a symbol of preparation for our trip. It's how we feel secure, prepared, and in control of our experience even before we get there. We're convinced that if we just have the right things with us, it'll be great. Maybe the airlines push you to travel light by adding fees for carry-on bags and limiting the size and weight of your luggage, but it seems like everyone else subscribes to the "More is more" philosophy. It's like if you don't think of it now and you don't bring it with you, your trip will be a failure and there's nothing you'll be able to do to redeem it. That mindset is what keeps us riddled with packing anxiety, scouring the internet for tips, and beating ourselves up again and again if we forget something, as if we've failed personally. But this is where, as solo travelers, we find ourselves in a losing battle. If you bring everything you're told to bring, you may think you've won—until you try dragging your suitcase up a four-story walk-up. Then you'll realize the other side of solo travel—you have to carry everything yourself, too.

So, in this chapter, I'm going to give you some of my favorite packing tips. Some have to do with what you should put in your suitcase (and possibly more importantly, what you think you need but actually don't). But some won't go into your suitcase at all—they're ideas and concepts that will make you a stronger and better solo traveler overall.

SPOILER ALERT: YOU DON'T NEED EVERYTHING

Once on a trip with my infant daughter, I had a total packing meltdown. Let me tell you, packing your own stuff is one thing; travel packing for a baby is a whole other. There's the car seat, of course. And the stroller. And the pack-and-play (for bedtime and naps). Baby-size clothes and a blanket. Diapers—if you go through five in a day, that's thirty-five diapers in a week. Two packages of wipes. Baby snacks, a breast pump and bottles, or both. And what about mealtime? The baby will need something to sit in, right? Enter the travel highchair, and…well, you can see how that list gets pretty intense. By the end of it all, I wondered if I should just stay home.

There was a point, though, when I came to a realization. Nora didn't need all those things. She needed only a few of them—namely, a few diapers and wipes. When I traveled with her to Madrid at six months old, she slept on a cozy blanket on the floor. I nursed her rather than bringing bottles (a luxury for some I know, but a possibility for me). And we took public transportation everywhere, so I just wore her in a baby carrier, ditched the bulky car seat and stroller, and brought an umbrella stroller as backup. It turns out that with all the cobblestones (especially during our day trip to the charming town of Toledo), I didn't use the stroller much anyway.

The thing I realized during that time—and this is a lesson for all of us, not just for people with kids—is that every country has babies. What I mean by this is that regular everyday people live everyday regular lives everywhere you are going (unless you're camping or backpacking or something like that, in which case you'll need to pack with a little more care). They need snacks and ibuprofen and sunscreen and umbrellas and contact solution and all sorts of things just like you do. While it's important to pack things that you know you'll need, you don't need to beat yourself up about remembering every little thing. You may realize there wasn't a whole lot you really needed after all that you couldn't buy in your destination (or if not that exact product, then a local solution that solves your need perhaps in a way you never even considered). Snacks are my favorite example of this. Once on a Wanderful trip, a woman brought a suitcase filled top to bottom with granola bars. She was terrified she would get hungry. She had completely forgotten that there were many awesome and delicious local snack options in her destination. In fact, finding new snacks is one of my favorite little details of traveling somewhere.

What you bring is only one very small part of your travel experience. In fact, you could lose your entire suitcase and still find that you can have an amazing trip—people have lived to tell that tale (it's also a great reason to make sure your essentials, like medication, are *always* packed in your carry-on). At the end of the day, stuff is stuff. How's that for traveling light?

ONE MUST: YOUR TRUSTED TRAVEL JOURNAL (SHE'S BACK!)

Packing for a solo trip is a huge anxiety, and if there's anyone who can help with that, it's the handy-dandy travel journal you've grown to know and love. Maybe on one of your pretravel experiences you already thought about what you should have brought with you; maybe you even took the time to jot it down.

(A light jacket when you got a little chilly out in that kayak? A small power bank when your phone battery ran low?)

Maybe your journal is simply a space for you to reflect on where that anxiety is coming from if you're feeling it. What do you fear will happen if you go on this trip unprepared? What are some of the ways you can address that now so if you do forget something, you're in a better spot?

Your travel journal is also a great place to write a packing list for yourself. If you're a fan of lists (like I am), you'll find their double utility: Not only can you do a brain dump of everything you *think* you need, but you can also take the time to edit it down to what you *actually* need. When you take a moment to think through your packing list in advance, you give yourself the freedom to actually assess if there is a better solution you haven't thought of. And one of those solutions might be not bringing that item at all.

THE GOLDEN RULES: BRING HALF OR USE ALL

I'm not going to spend a lot of time walking through the exact checklists of what items to bring on your trip, though I will give you some favorites. I also want to leave you with a few general rules. You just learned a few of them already—that what you pack is not always directly proportional to how successful your trip will be and that there are many things you can buy abroad because you're (most likely) traveling to a place where people live.

But I'll give you a more direct packing tip, especially when it comes to clothes and shoes. It's to bring half and use all.

What does that mean, exactly? Let me explain.

A key to traveling solo is packing as lightly as you can. We've established that you're going to be carrying a lot of stuff, so you want your suitcase or backpack to be as portable as possible so you're not getting dragged down. As you think about what you need, remind yourself of the importance of reusing or using up. You likely actually need only about half of what you think you need, because some of the things you're bringing can be reused or reworn. Plan to use things up fully, so that when you come home your stock is pretty much depleted. The more you use up, the more room you'll have to take things home with you if you want them.

If you're traveling for six days, you do not need six outfits. Bring three shirts and three pants. Or three dresses. Plan to rewear everything once. Bring a small bar of laundry soap if the idea of rewearing something terrifies you. *Bring half.*

If you're bringing your own hair products, try squeezing the amount you need into a portable travel bottle so that you're not carrying an entire bottle (and all that weight) with you. *Use all.*

If you're throwing something in at the last minute "just in case" (a pair of heels "just in case" you get invited to a nice event, maybe?), rethink your choice. Find an alternative, like a pair of flats that you *know* you'll use regardless (and that fit easier into your suitcase, to boot). "Just in case" should be a red flag—it means you will most likely not need it. If you hear yourself say it, stop and reevaluate whether there's something you know you'll use that you can also use for a "just in case" moment. *Use all.*

When you're packing your bag, you should ask yourself:

- Am I *definitely* going to need this, or just *possibly*? *Use all.*
- Is this a consumable product that I'm going to use only part of, like a full-size bottle of shampoo? *Use all.*

215

- Can I reuse this, or wash it, rather than bringing extras? *Bring half.*
- If I'm traveling for a long period of time, is it better to ship any of these items to my destination instead rather than carry them? *Bring half.*

The Exceptions

Even knowing that, by and large, you could purchase or replace many of the things you'd be packing, there are a few items you might want to prioritize bringing. Those include:

- Special toiletry products, especially if you have a hair or skin type that is not part of the dominant race or culture in your destination or if you're using any medicated hair or skin treatments.
- Medications, including hormones and birth control. Many medical insurances will cover the advance purchase of prescription medication specifically for travel. Make sure that it is still in its original packaging and that you have a copy of the prescription with you at all times. Bring an ice pack or thermos if it needs to stay cool. Don't forget to check the expiration date before traveling with it.
- An extra pair of prescription glasses or contacts, which might be hard to get on the fly.
- A tiny first aid kit. Yes, you can buy Band-Aids abroad. But do you really want to have to run to the store after you realize you need one? Bringing a few bandages, some hand sanitizer, and a couple of ibuprofen or Excedrin could make all the difference and won't take up a whole lot of space in your pack.
- If you have severe dietary restrictions, allergies, or a condition such as diabetes—yes, bring snacks! Don't take my

"Buy local snacks" advice for gospel, especially if you're going to a place where you might be concerned about the contents or preparation of what you're eating. I guarantee that you do not need to pack an entire suitcase of granola bars, but it may help to bring some things to tide you over until you find a local solution.

LET'S TALK ABOUT FASHION

Time for some real talk: How trendy do you actually need to be on your solo trip? With the "Instagrammification" of travel, not only have we been obsessed with perfect, edited travel photos, but we have also become more accustomed to seeing these same photos featuring a protagonist wearing a super-trendy outfit or a billowing evening gown. Even if we don't have aspirations to be influencers ourselves, it does make us question if we should be sharing travel photos when we're obviously wearing the same outfit in various different shots.

So that brings you to the question: Should you actually rewear your clothing? Sure, it sounds like a good idea on the surface (more room in your suitcase = lighter load = better travel experience overall, right?). Of course, your ability to rewear an outfit is going to depend on your trip, the weather, the amount you sweat (seriously, though), how clean the clothing is, and your overall willingness to do it. If you're visiting Angkor Wat in hundred-degree heat, you might not want to wear that same tank top over again. But as I've mentioned above, a good stick of laundry soap and a clean sink can do wonders.

Everyone has a different tolerance level for this, of course. I'll happily rewear clothing that's still clean. This would be mortifying to some people and, as always, this is *your* trip. You do you. But before you go buying an entirely new wardrobe, I want to remind you of a couple of things.

First, don't feel the need to dress any "trendier" than you would at home. What you wear and who you are is enough. You are traveling for you—not for the pictures, and certainly not for anyone else. You want to feel comfortable in your own skin, and sometimes the best way to do that is just by wearing what makes you feel most at ease with yourself. Often my gift to myself on solo trips is local accessories, so I'll purposely bring very little with me from home, instead opting for a more basic range of clothing articles that I can dress up with locally purchased items. Choosing simple base layers and complementing them with accessories (whether that's jewelry or hats and scarves) gives you a dual benefit: You can choose to "blend in" when you want (which for some is a safety precaution), and then you can opt to express yourself more loudly, too, without having to make a major wardrobe change. You'd be surprised how versatile jeans and a top, or a simple cotton dress, can be with the right accents.

Respecting local culture is also important. If you're traveling to a conservative area, make sure you bring conservative clothing. This is also where working the base layer/accessory strategy has magic—a scarf can cover shoulders and knees in a pinch. If you're worried that your destination is just many times cooler and trendier than you, and your mere fashion sense will expose you as a foreigner, those accessories you pick up locally will serve the dual purpose of helping you meet your expectations for yourself while giving you a great souvenir to take home and reuse.

Leave the Most Meaningful Items at Home

What would happen if you lost your grandmother's necklace, or your engagement ring, or that drawing you keep folded in your wallet that your now-grown son made for you when he was four? Even if the items aren't worth a whole lot in a financial sense, if they have sentimental value, don't bring them. Before you pack anything, always think to yourself, *If I were to lose this item on a trip, would I be devastated?* If the answer is yes, spare yourself the anxiety and leave it at home.

OKAY, BUT THERE ARE SOME THINGS...

There are a few items that almost always make it onto my packing list. Get out your highlighter, because trust me, once you travel with them, you'll never want to go back:

- **A scarf.** It should open into a large square. This is the most versatile piece of travel gear you'll own. You can use it as a blanket when you're cold on a bus. You can wrap it around your shoulders when you're in the Vatican, around your waist like a sarong when you're at the beach, or over your head when you're in a mosque. You can open it and sit on it for that impromptu park picnic. You can also use it as padding for that really pretty Moroccan lantern you just have to bring home, even though you know it'll probably break in the suitcase. Or...you can even wear it as a scarf!

- **A maxi dress.** I could basically live in maxi dresses. They're irresistibly comfortable. They're breezy enough for summer travel and warm enough for winter (ideally with a pair of leggings underneath). They're great for curling up on a plane, giving you breathability and freedom, and can double as a blanket. They provide coverage in more conservative places, especially when paired with a long-sleeved top or cardigan. And they are completely forgiving after that seven-course prix fixe menu. If dresses aren't your thing, a jumpsuit or romper is an excellent alternative.

- **A good pair of flats.** I love heels, but as I said above, unless you have a *really* good reason and know *for sure* that you'll wear them multiple times (for example, if you're traveling specifically for an event), leave the heels at home. They're completely impractical and they take up a lot of luggage space. Bring a couple of good pairs of flats that you feel comfortable in: Sneakers for a day of walking, sandals to give the toes a break, and some ballet flats are about all I need for a wide variety of experiences.

- **Light, interchangeable layers.** We can all agree it's pretty easy to pack for warm weather because clothing is generally less bulky. But if you're traveling during a cold season, it can be a lot more challenging. One warm, chunky sweater can fill half a carry-on suitcase pretty quickly. That's where layers become even more important. Pay attention to fabric choices, so that each layer performs at its best. Wool and synthetics will keep you warmer and more comfortable after a day of cold rain than cotton, which can stay cold and wet longer. Maximize your rewearing strategy so that you get the most use out of your layers. Wear the chunkiest thing on the plane (it's usually cold in there anyway). If you want a "just in case" dress, try throwing in some bold, inexpensive statement jewelry to dress up or down that travel maxi dress or romper you brought, and you can skip bringing "something nice" entirely.

- **A reliable suitcase and a cross-body day bag.** When you're traveling alone, what you put your belongings *in* is arguably just as important as what you pack. A light and durable spinner suitcase (i.e., one with four wheels) will make all the difference when you're schlepping it around an airport. If you're going to be walking on a lot of uneven terrain, a strong and durable backpack with a good zipper is a worthy investment. During the day, a cross-body bag will give you all the space you need for your items while also sitting securely on your shoulder, which will also be less accessible to pickpockets.

Pro Tip: Luggage on the Go

If you're spending a day somewhere en route to another place, there are fantastic luggage storage solutions that solve the problem of carrying bags through a whole city. Stasher and LuggageHero are the more popular ones, which allow you to pay by the hour for local businesses to store your luggage for you. You may also benefit from some of the "pre-tech" luggage storage solutions—some museums will hold your luggage for free, and you'll get the benefit of a museum day out of it. Some train stations also have large holding areas for luggage. Take a minute to preplan where your suitcase will go so you don't have to keep it with you all day.

- **A plane kit.** If you've got a long plane ride, getting restful sleep on it is not just important; it's pretty much essential. That's why I bring a small "plane kit" with me wherever I go, but especially on flights that are longer than three hours.

Inside are fuzzy warm socks (yes, happy feet = happy people); an eye mask (because sometimes you need to nap and the plane lights will be on); a sleep aid (mine includes diphenhydramine, which is essentially a light-dose Benadryl, but you may enjoy something natural like lavender); and earbuds. I'll also bring a neck pillow, which may feel like a luxury with so much to carry, but it really does make a difference for me. Get one with snaps so that you can clip it around a backpack or suitcase. Some people swear by inflatable pillows, though I haven't found one that's comfortable enough for me yet.

- **And finally…something fun you can do with others.** One of my most favorite things to bring with me on a solo trip is a set of nail polishes. It sounds funny, but let me tell you something—when I'm by myself in a small town and I'm sitting at a café or by a fountain and I whip out a set of nail polishes and start doing my nails, you better believe I'm going to make some friends. It's an instant way to connect with others, and it gives you something easy to talk about; or if you're staying with a host family, it's a fun activity you can do together. I've seen other people use the same concept in other ways—maybe you're a good chef and you bring some specialty ingredients from home to cook in your hostel or homestay. Maybe you can juggle or do card tricks. Maybe you play the piano (I fully recognize you may not bring your own piano, but in my experience, people who play piano have the magical ability to find pianos just about everywhere). Anything that you can do with someone else or teach to someone else instantly creates connection that you don't need language for.

While there are some things that are always on my list whenever I'm traveling (and especially traveling alone), also keep in mind that the details of what you'll need are always different depending on the place you're traveling to and the activities that you're doing there. Your suitcase is going to look a lot different if you're skiing in the Swiss Alps than if you're gorilla trekking in Uganda or urban backpacking in Seoul. There are tons of great packing resources out there, and a quick Google search can usually point you in the direction you need to go for your type of trip and destination and the unique needs of those places.

SAFETY, YOUR PERIOD, AND OTHER "GIRL STUFF"

In 2012, Bic (the pen company) created Bic for Her—a line of pens that was advertised as "elegant design—just for her!" and with a "thin barrel to fit a woman's hand." The internet went wild. "FINALLY a tool for me to use to shatter that pesky glass ceiling—and it's PINK! Thanks, boys!" said one reviewer called Robin. "What I appreciate most is the ultra lightweight feel of this pen in my hand, especially during that time of the month when you almost can't be bothered to get out of bed in the morning," noted Fleur de Lisa.[1]

In case you missed it, these reviews are all sarcastic—because, come on, do we really need special pens that fit a woman's hand?

Products designed for women are a double-edged sword. On the one hand, we've lived in a world that hasn't even considered our needs for a very long time. But now we're living in a world where creating a "girly" version of everything seems like a reasonable alternative (at least initially). Holiday gift guides can sometimes feel cringe-worthy—we share the best gifts for women in travel, which often tend to be feminine versions of other perfectly useful travel products.

There are a few exceptions to this, and they largely fall into two categories: safety products and menstrual products. While you all know how I feel at this point about the complicated world of women's travel safety, I do think there are some great products out there that may set your mind more at ease, especially depending on your personal risk profile. Here are some worth investigating:

Safety Products

- Travel bras and infinity scarves with secret pockets for you to store valuables like your passport and money
- Pickpocket-proof clothing, which features a combination of zippers that make it difficult for a pickpocket to pick on the fly
- Portable door locks, which are particularly useful when you're in a hostel or shared living environment
- Safety jewelry, which can call emergency numbers when triggered
- Safety apps that make an emergency call when you press a button on your phone

Period Products

- Menstrual cups, which users swear by, can be washed and reused, and save you tons of space in your luggage

- Period panties, which are often used in combination with another period product during heavier periods but are meant to be used alone
- Birth control reminder apps, especially ones that are time-zone friendly (they also work as general prescription medication reminders)

There are so many great brands building and innovating for women, many of which are women-led. You can find some specific recommendations in the Resources sections at the end of this book. But ultimately know this: You do you. Safety gadgets are great and may make you feel at ease, but they're not everything. While period products have made some amazing headway in recent years, make sure you try them out and like them before taking them on your trip. Assessing your needs, and your comfort, is of utmost importance.

SO...DID I BRING THE FAKE ENGAGEMENT RING?

Everyone wants to know, right?

In the end, I did bring the fake engagement ring. I even wore it once or twice, and I'll be honest—there was a marked difference between the number of times I got hit on when I was wearing the ring and when I wasn't. But a gaudy fake engagement ring might be overkill, and make you a target for pickpockets, especially if it does look real. Now that I'm married, I bring a plain wedding band with me and leave my expensive jewelry at home. If you're worried about attention, wearing a simple band on your finger may be enough.

At the end of the day, there is no one thing on your trip that is going to make or break your solo adventure. For the most part, anything left behind can be purchased abroad. Anything that can't be purchased abroad you will simply go without. Maybe it'll be a lesson learned and an opportunity to jot a note in your travel journal—or maybe you'll realize you didn't actually need it after all.

The items you carry in your backpack (or your suitcase) are tools to make your journey easier, not harder. But the most important tools aren't ones that you carry in your luggage at all. They're the lessons (and yes, the mindset) that you bring with you on this journey in the first place: to give yourself grace, to go with the flow, and to embrace opportunities to go local (even unexpected opportunities). Lucky for you, none of those lessons weigh a thing, so you can bring all of them along.

Chapter 11

WELCOME TO DAY ZERO

"Loving life is easy when you are abroad. Where no one knows you and you hold your life in your hands all alone, you are more master of yourself than at any other time."

—Hannah Arendt

AH...HERE WE ARE.

Maybe you're reading this chapter while you're sitting at the airport. Your bags are packed, set beside you or being loaded into the belly of your plane. You feel that anticipation, those little butterflies in your stomach. You hear the announcements overhead of boarding, gate changes, last calls. Thousands of people going on thousands of their own adventures, and now you're one of them.

Maybe you're at the train station, feeling the light wind through the tunnel as your train approaches. You grip your boarding pass tightly (or maybe it's just your phone nowadays), your lifeline. Maybe it's a bus station. You're standing there and you're waiting in anticipation for the journey to begin.

Maybe you're still just dreaming of that day. You're thinking about what it will feel like, what it will look like. Will it be sunny? Raining? Will you cry? Will you back out? Will you feel calm and ready to leave when the time comes? Will you throw up in an airport bathroom from sheer nerves?

If there are two confidence jumps you need to take during your solo trip, the first one is booking that flight. But the second one is that moment of departure. The most stress and anticipation I feel in my trip is in the gearing up to go. Packing my things. Saying goodbye to my loved ones. Scheduling my Lyft and timing it perfectly so I both manage Boston traffic and don't spend *too* long waiting at the airport. Going through security and peeking at the line (speaking of which, if you already know you're planning for a lot of travel to and from the US, a Global Entry pass will make your life a thousand times less stressful, if only for the included TSA Precheck).

Once I'm past security, though, my concerns evaporate. I feel light and calm. I have a plan. I trust myself. I'm already set in motion, and the easier thing at this point is to just let inertia carry me forward. I pull up a book on my tablet or buy one at the bookstore. In fact, if it's your first trip, I recommend you give yourself a little extra time at the airport and just *enjoy it*. Sit down and have a meal (this is actually one of the few places you'll see *lots* of people dining at sit-down restaurants alone). Or peruse the bookstore and actually thumb through pages of publications or periodicals. Or get a chair massage. Or pick up a new travel journal if your other one is already full and take some time to write and reflect in it. Let yourself have time at the airport to be still and to relish this first moment with your-self while still in your home country. Can you already feel your molecules changing?

There is only so much we can do to psyche ourselves up about traveling alone. We can plan it. We can research our trip. We can talk it up with our friends. We can buy all sorts of new gear and gadgets. We can start that travel blog. But there's a certain moment—that moment of lift—when you just need to trust yourself and jump. It's also in that moment when you learn how much you can really fly.

Getting to that point of departure may feel like one of the bravest things you could do, but guess what? You've done it already. If you practiced your pretravel regimen—eating out alone, going on a day trip, or even taking a weekend away—you've already taken a solo trip. You're not a first-timer any-more. The pool may be a little deeper, but it's still a pool. You might be swimming a little more, but you're still swimming.

―――――――Z―――――――

Just as we learned that travel can manifest itself in different ways and that you don't need to dive into the deep end of a trip first, I also want you to think about those first few moments of your arrival—the moments when you hop off the plane (or train or motorcycle or catamaran or whatever mode of trans-port you're taking), take a moment to scan the world around you, and think, *Okay, what's next?*

Those first few moments of getting off the plane are always a mad dash. Everyone grabs their bags, crowds the aisles, races to Passport Control, pulls their suitcases off the carousel at bag-gage claim, and they're off to somewhere. But you're in no rush.

A lot of pressure has built up to this moment—this moment when you realize you are *actually doing the thing* and *need to make the most of every minute*. You may feel like you need to match the speed of the people around you and rush out the exit. You may feel like you need to drop your bags quickly at your hotel and immediately find the closest trendy hotspot and snap a selfie. But actually, you don't need to do any of that. You don't owe this moment anything. In fact, that's why one of my top recommendations for solo travelers is to not start your trip with a Day One, but a Day Zero.

WHAT IS A DAY ZERO?

If Day One is the first day of really leaning in and experiencing a place, Day Zero is the prequel. It's the Wednesday food prep before Thanksgiving, when you're chopping brussels sprouts and brining the turkey. It's the spa day before your best friend's wedding, when you're getting your nails done. Day Zero is the day before your exam that you spend resting and watching Netflix, the team pasta night before tomorrow's big sports game. The difference here is that you don't experience Day Zero *before* your trip; you experience it on the day of arrival. This is for two reasons: The first is because you'll want to give your body time to rest and recover after your travels and in anticipation of the busy day(s) ahead, especially if you're acclimating to a new time zone. The second is because you will want to be fully immersed in your surroundings so that you can begin to adjust, slowly and smoothly, with no schedule and no plan. Day Zero is the day when you just show up in a place and your whole job is to rest up, settle in, and observe what's around you, with no expectations and no itinerary.

There's a lot to recognize on Day Zero, especially on Day Zero of a first solo trip. You may have already started to notice some of the things we've talked about in earlier chapters—a change in the air related to the culture of your current location. You might still be in the airport and yet begin to notice differences in how other women are dressed or the presence of women at all. You might be very conscious of how much you stand out due to your skin or hair color, even here where there is a mix of people from around the world. Sometimes the airport feels like the depressurized chamber of a space station before going on a space walk, or the entryway before a butterfly garden where you have to sit for a minute so the butterflies don't all fly out. You're in that place between where you were before and where you're going now. We don't give enough attention to that moment of transition, but here you are: a new goldfish swimming in a plastic bag, acclimating to the temperature of its new aquarium before the bag opens. That's you, halfway into this new space, seeing the differences while still holding on to the comfort of the place you were in seemingly moments ago. Knowing that as soon as those airport doors slide open, you're free.

The airport may not feel like the place to have a self-care moment, but just as you took time for yourself on your departure, let yourself have that moment upon your arrival, too. Don't rush to baggage claim. Linger awhile. There is so much to celebrate about this moment. This is your first day in new territory. You are in complete control of yourself. You might have thought you were in control of yourself at home, and you probably were. But the context of your life—your friendships, your responsibilities, your routines—created a rhythm for you, and now you have an opportunity to explore an entirely different beat. You may feel pressure to start here and now at 100 miles per hour. But this is where Day Zero becomes your secret weapon, your solo travel superpower. Day Zero reminds you that today, all you have to do is *be*.

While your first goal is to get your body caught up to your new surroundings, it's also an important day for getting your bearings. As a solo traveler, you have to rely on yourself for just about everything. You don't have the luxury of another person who can casually comment to you, "Oh, I noticed a really cool restaurant down the street where we should have drinks." YOU need to be the person who notices that cute restaurant. You don't have someone who can say, "I saw someone fill a plastic card at this station in order to use the subway." YOU have to figure out the local transit and how it works. And because of that, it's extra important to take a moment to just sit back and observe. It'll take care of the dual task of giving yourself time to settle in, while also giving you information and context that will make the rest of your trip smoother. Remember, if I had only taken a Day Zero on my trip to New Orleans, I would have figured out the local transit system and saved myself $150.

There are a lot of really brilliant ways to approach a Day Zero. Ultimately, it comes down to not planning anything, giving yourself time to adjust and observe, spending a few moments getting to know your new landing place, and making sure you rest and recover. The intent is to schedule almost nothing on Day Zero. Tempted as you may be to rush out and do the thing you've been dreaming of, anything that's on your bucket list should *not* be planned for Day Zero. Day Zero is specifically about being quite unplanned.

Now, that's not to say you don't do *anything* (unless that's your vibe, in which case, carry on, Wander Woman!), so let's take a look at a few tried-and-true Day Zero activities.

Explore Your Hotel and Take a Walk in the Daytime

This is as much a good travel tactic as a really good safety tactic. When you check into your hotel, don't drop your bags and rush out. Take some time to explore your immediate surroundings. Spend a moment chatting with the guest services team. Ride the elevator to different floors and see what's on them. I can't tell you the number of times I was about to leave a hotel only to realize upon checkout that there was a pool or a really stunning rooftop bar. *What was I even doing here?* I'd wonder, displeased with myself. Same goes for an Airbnb, a hostel, or a homestay: Read the house rules, open all the cupboards, find the extra towels, and check to see if the hairdryer works. Or find the water hookups for your RV or the bear-proof food locker. Unpack and let your curiosity guide you.

Once you've gotten a good grip on where you're staying, have a stroll around your neighborhood. Use this as an opportunity to be really observant. What does it actually look like—the buildings, the road, the sidewalk? Where is your hotel in relation to other things (it's also a really good time to write down that hotel address on paper in case you haven't done that yet)? What's across the street from you?

Take your time and mosey. See if you can identify a market or supermarket nearby. Try to look for signs of public transportation and how people use it or where they buy a ticket or pass.

Remember that your surroundings will look different at night. What landmarks can you point out and remember for later? What other pieces of information could be useful to you for navigation?

Once you start to get those bearings, you'll be able to increase your situational awareness without having to constantly be on the lookout for where you are. You'll have familiarity with your place and the ability to feel more comfortable in your current home base. That will be immensely helpful later, if only because it'll save you a lot of time figuring that out when you actually have somewhere to be.

Stop by the Tourism Office or Visitors Center

Have you been to a tourism office or visitors center lately? Some of them are massive spaces with stacks and stacks of brochures. I stopped by the Kansas City, Missouri, tourism office and it literally looks like someone's apartment, complete with a kitchen and a TV/lounge area. However they look, they all function the same way: They want to make sure you have the best time in their city.

Stopping by the tourism office is a great opportunity to pick up lots of brochures. (This is also something you should do at the airport, if you're okay with consuming paper. I love to grab a few brochures to read at a café later.) Take them with you, or just read through them there. But don't solely rely on the brochures—take some time to talk to the local tourism rep, too. Not only can they help recommend great things to do, but they can also give you good insight into places that align with your values, like locally owned, as well as women- and minority-owned businesses. In Edinburgh, Scotland, tourism reps literally walk around the floor like an Apple Store, asking visitors if they have questions and making recommendations.

Sometimes the newer and smaller businesses don't make it into the print brochures, so talking to a local is key. They know because they live there—and also because, well, it's kind of their job to know.

In a way, let the tourism office be your secret sauce. They're locals who love their city, and they want to make sure you love it, too.

Find a Café and People-Watch

Take those brochures with you from the tourism office to a nearby café (in fact, here's an opportunity to ask your tourism rep about a favorite café nearby!). See if you can find one with outdoor seating if it's warm so you can watch people and see where they're going. Make up fun stories about them in your head. Write in your travel journal. Eat a sandwich. Have a cup of coffee (you probably need it). Take an opportunity to order something that looks different and new. Pick up a newspaper and read it if you can. Read through those travel brochures and circle stuff that looks interesting. Give yourself a mental and physical break and just be present in the place you're in before you spend a lot of energy exploring. This is the moment you're here for—the moment to immerse yourself in something new. Take it in.

Visit the Grocery Store

I'll admit, I'm a bit of an introvert when I first arrive in a new place. I'm tired. I don't want to talk to anyone. I wish I could say I'm the most totally game, talk-to-strangers, show-up-at-a-random-person's-Pakistani-wedding kind of traveler on Day Zero, but I'm not. I feel out of place, and I don't have my bearings yet. The French call this *dépaysement*, a feeling of disorientation and betweenness. You might feel that way, too. That's why one of my favorite Day Zero activities is to visit the grocery store.

It might be a supermarket. It might be a farmers market. But find a place where people do their daily or weekly grocery shopping. Then...take all the time you want. Walk through the cereal aisle and gaze at the children's TV characters that you don't recognize. Go through the produce section and have a look at what kinds of veggies are local. Gawk at the strange flavors of chips. Marvel over the fact that wine can be cheaper than water in Bulgaria, or follow your nose to the ridiculous stink of the giant fillets of dried, salted cod that take up an impressive section of Portuguese grocery stores (don't worry, you'll smell them before you see them).

You will feel nearly invisible in a grocery store, in a good way. It will give you that moment of absolutely no pressure. Of relief. But you'll also get a chance to try some new things—and fill your belly. Pick up some snacks and take them back to the hotel room and have a picnic for yourself. Explore your new city through new flavors that you may never have tasted before.

Bonus: Have Dinner with a Buddy

If you're a little bit more of a social butterfly, you might want to make a dinner plan for tonight. Having dinner with a local is a great way to get a little bit of a private orientation to your new place while also refueling your tank. You might not know who that buddy is yet—it's not your job to have a friend in every part of the world—but luckily that problem is solved for you, too.

Hop on Meetup.com and see if anything is happening in your area tonight. Sign up for an Eatwith or a Traveling Spoon (these are websites where you can pay for a spot at someone's dinner table, kind of like Airbnb for meals). If you're part of the Wanderful network, you'll know that there are thousands of women waiting to connect with you and show you their city, their home. So why not prearrange a dinner date with someone on your first night? Use it as a chance to get settled in, to not have to think about what you'll eat (I would literally tell them to pick the place), and ask loads of questions with a friendly travel lover who's literally just there to be a support system. If you're still not sure about eating alone, it's a great way to ease into that first day slowly and with a local hand to hold. Plus, along the way you'll get lots of good advice on what to do for the rest of your trip.

Hire a Photographer

I know this sounds like a pretty silly Day Zero activity, and maybe you're just *too* tired to get glammed up and actually do it, but I've found hiring a local photographer is an amazing way to get an introduction to a place with a local as well as get some really good travel photos for your trip (it's also one of my favorite ways to invest in the local economy, one of my suggestions back in chapter 6). Remember, you're going to be taking a lot of selfies—so you might find it worthwhile to invest an hour or two to have some nice photos *of* you, rather than just those taken *by* you.

The thing I really love about hiring a local photographer is that they already know their city and its prettiest parts, and they've seen it through a photographer's eyes. There's a lot you can do with just yourself and a photographer for an hour (no kids to try to pose or large groups to manage), so I recommend you invite them to take the reins and decide where you should go and just follow their whim. I'd also use the opportunity to ask them questions about how to get around, what *their* favorite restaurant is, and what to see.

You may think that finding a local photographer is a lot of work, but sites like Flytographer, which is woman-founded, connect you with local photographers in cities around the world, making it remarkably easy to pick someone you like, contact them, and book online. If you want to do a traditional Day Zero and not plan anything, this is also a great Day One activity.

Sign Up for a Walking Tour

Walking tours are one of my favorite Day Zero activities, and like the recommendation above, they could be designated for a good Day One if you want a real Day Zero of absolutely no planning. Regardless, put a walking tour at the top of your list of things to do before planning anything else. It's a fun way to get the "lay of the land" from a local. Not only do you get to see some of the top sights, but you also have a person you can ask all those questions that you've had, like "I keep seeing this green sign everywhere—what does it mean?" or "How do you say 'Thank you' in the local language?"

Lucky for you, there are tons of great walking tours to choose from. The local visitors center can help—that's how I found a free Sandemans tour in Tel Aviv departing in just thirty minutes. Lots of hostels and hybrids also offer tours for their guests. If you're looking to schedule a tour in advance, there are tons of walking tour companies available, from completely private ones, to larger group ones, to food tours, which kick things up a notch by adding a satisfying gastronomic element. Not only do you get a quick introduction to your destination, but you also don't have to figure out what you'll eat for dinner. That's self-care at its finest.

Do Something Completely Normal, Even Boring

I want to give you another good solo travel lesson that I learned through the eyes of my favorite traveling companion (and your favorite object of humor, my loving husband, Marvin).

It was 2014 and we were on a plane to Istanbul, Türkiye. We were visiting Istanbul for exactly twenty-four hours, travel-hacking our way to a much cheaper trip to the Greek Islands, which we found we could do by visiting Istanbul for an overnight and then taking a short hop over to Greece, rather than flying direct. We were traveling for a wedding but were excited to add in a couple of jaunts of our own.

It was our first time visiting Istanbul. We had a very, very long list of things to do in a short period of time: Visit the Hagia Sophia. Check out the Blue Mosque. Try shisha. And visit Topkapi Palace, if we could squeeze it in.

Our plane touched down and I was everything but pulling out my checklist, ready to hit the ground running.

Marvin turned to me and said, "Can I get a haircut first?"

I stopped and looked at him. I couldn't see my own face, but I'm pretty sure it was a mix of completely awestruck and dumbfounded. Was the guy freaking serious? We just flew thousands of miles for a once-in-a-lifetime twenty-four-hour adventure in Türkiye and he WANTED TO GET A HAIRCUT?!

Marvin begged; he reaaaally wanted to look good for the wedding, and he hadn't had time to do it before we left.

I grimaced and groaned. We had so little time, and where on earth were we going to find a barber? We didn't even know what a barbershop looked like in Türkiye, or if people there were even accustomed to Marvin's hair type as a Black man.

Marvin won the argument.

Two hours later, we'd dropped our bags at our hotel and then found ourselves walking in the Sultanahmet District. We walked down a street, and Marvin's barber spidey senses took charge. We turned off onto a side road, then we turned off onto another side road. He spotted an old man standing outside what looked like a tiny hole-in-the-wall shop. He looked at the man, made the universal "scissors" motion, and the man nodded and retreated inside.

We followed him into the smallest barbershop you've ever seen. It was narrow and dark. On the walls were old newspaper clippings and photographs of that same barber posing with various people, I assumed local and national celebrities. There were two chairs; the barber motioned for me to sit in one, Marvin in the other. He then, without hesitation, began to cut Marvin's hair. At one point he took a cotton ball, lit it on fire, and used it to lightly singe the hairs off Marvin's outer ears. Let me say that again: FIRE was used as a tool in this haircut.

When he finished, Marvin had a seriously good haircut, and my jaw was pretty much on the floor.

That. Was. The. Coolest. Thing. I. Have. Ever. SEEN!

Imagine what would have happened had Marvin not turned to me and asked for a haircut. We would have seen some pretty neat sights, sure. We would have had some other interesting experiences exploring a really stunning castle or some additional history. But how many of you can tell the story of visiting a Turkish barbershop—let alone a tiny, been-around-for-fifty-years one—and watching a haircut up close? Smelling the burn of a cotton ball lit on fire? Watching old black-and-white Turkish TV with a guy who's probably cut thousands of heads of hair in his lifetime? It was interesting, different, and unique. It was a completely banal, everyday experience—but as a traveler, sometimes those boring, everyday experiences are the ones that really stand out, because the differences stand out.

Day Zero isn't *just* about resting, or even about getting your bearings. Sometimes Day Zero can serve as a reminder to us that many of the best moments and memories are the ones that we could never plan, because we choose to look at the world with wonder; we look at totally normal, everyday life with fresh eyes. And we let ourselves be open to the possibility that in a new context, and alone with ourselves, we can begin to see things differently than we ever have before.

Chapter 12

YOU ARE DIFFERENT AND THE SAME

"I think you travel to search and you come back home to find yourself there."

—Chimamanda Ngozi Adichie

HAVE YOU HEARD OF THE FOURTH TRIMESTER? IT'S A PREG-nancy term that refers to the three months *after* a baby is born. While all the baby books out there spend a lot of time preparing expectant parents for pregnancy and labor, it seems like everything that happens after labor just sort of fades to black. There is disturbingly little information related to the physical changes that happen to a body after giving birth, as well as the emotional changes that happen to someone when they become responsible for another life. It's why some will argue that the fourth trimester is the most important one, even though it's talked about the least.

Your trip is not dissimilar in this respect. There are thousands upon thousands of resources about how to plan the perfect trip. You'll get some amazing advice on the ground about what to do during your travels. But very few people talk about coming home, as if when you return home, everything you experience dissipates and you revert to normal. That's a problem, because the return—the feeling of going back to "life as it was," of processing what you experienced abroad, and the sometimes-emotional roller coaster that can follow you back—can be one of the most fundamentally life-changing parts of your trip, and most of us don't expect it.

We call this process of returning "reentry," or sometimes "reverse culture shock," and if there's anyone who's an expert on it, it's Dr. Cate Brubaker. Dr. Cate is the creator of Small Planet Studio, a company that is dedicated entirely to the topic of reentry. She has helped thousands of people manage and process their experiences returning home and has published amazing tools like a reentry tool kit for study abroad and a reentry road-map workbook. She does this because she herself experienced a complicated process of reentry and didn't have the resources she needed to tackle it head-on. So she developed some.

"No one talks about reentry beyond reverse culture shock," she explains. "They always assume that reentry is just the first couple of weeks. It's going to the grocery store and being overwhelmed by the number of cereal brands we have. When reverse culture shock ends, people think, 'Oh, I'm done; I'm good.' But that's when reentry actually begins."

Reentry isn't just about being surprised by how different your home is from another place that you may have gotten used to. It's also about being surprised by how you have changed. It's about trying to integrate all that we've seen and done into our regular life when no one around us has had that same experience. Everyone goes through reentry to some degree, but the degree to which you struggle with it will depend on a multitude of factors: from how long you were abroad to how far outside of your comfort zone you went while you were there and what types of weight you carried in your *mental backpack* (Dr. Cate's term), both before and after your trip. Usually, I find people experience a deeper level of reentry if they leave their home country, and in this chapter you'll see me reference international travel quite a bit. That does not, however, mean that reentry can't happen right within your home borders. The more you've challenged yourself to think differently, the fiercer the bite reentry will have when you return home. It's not like you pick it up only at Customs.

What I want you to take away from this chapter is the understanding that reentry is real and that it affects many of us, even the most experienced of travelers. I'll give you some tools to prepare for it, recognize it, and address it (in front of others as well as with yourself), but I want you to get used to sitting in its discomfort, too. The stronger you feel that dissonance, the more it means you've done the work to challenge yourself. Better said, it means you're growing.

YOU (AND THE REST OF THE WORLD)

There are two groups of people that you're going to have to reconcile your trip with. The first group is friends, family, or anyone who has been following along on your journey. You're going to have moments of frustration when they ask you questions, or want to know more about your experience, or when you find that your personality and some of the new things you've learned about yourself seem to clash with the person you were when you left.

The other person that you're going to have to reconcile this trip with is, well, *yourself*. For some of us that's even more challenging. Let's start with the "easy" ones first.

"HOW WAS YOUR TRIP?" OR, HOW TO APPROACH YOUR REENTRY WITH OTHERS

One of the most dreaded questions we travelers get is "How was your trip?"

It's great that people care about us and want to hear what we've been up to. But it can also be a really difficult question to answer, especially if you've done the work of getting uncomfortable, trying new things, and questioning yourself. It's hard to repackage the complex experience of traveling solo into something neat and tidy for your audience. You can say, "It was amazing!" and change the subject, but that feels incomplete. You can gush about all the delicious things you ate and all the sights you saw, but that sounds like bragging, and it also doesn't encapsulate the full breadth of challenging, moving, and complicated experiences you had. You can try to incorporate them, but be prepared to watch as your conversation mate's eyes begin to glaze over. You suddenly realize that they didn't actually want to know about your trip at all, and you've just spent the last twenty minutes monologuing about your convoluted feelings while they uncomfortably balanced a plate of now-cold mashed potatoes.

So…what's an answer that works for everyone (you, your conversation mate, and the world at large)?

Thinking about how you might answer this question *before* you return home can help you process your emotions and your trip ahead of time (so you're not live-processing them in front of an unsuspecting friend or family member). It's also why, if you choose to, sharing your experiences with others on a digital medium like a social media channel or a blog can be a nice way to allow them to follow along with your journey and have meaningful things to say when you return. And, of course, taking time to reflect in that handy travel journal gives you the space for more personal moments of processing.

Dr. Cate approaches the "How was your trip?" question all the time with her returnees, inviting them to focus on a few key moments that can shed light on their trip for others.

"I have them think about a few times while they were abroad that really stood out to them," she explains. "It could be funny, it could be challenging, it could be minor. I have them really think about and practice telling it, but also to think about what those moments mean to them. Sharing the meaning is what will connect you with the other person. They might not connect to the actual experience, but they'll connect with the meaning and they'll be interested in why that was meaningful to you."

It may feel impossible to fully encapsulate everything about your trip for everyone you talk to. And that's okay. I'm not sure there's ever going to be a way for you to communicate what you experienced and how it affected your worldview. Let yourself be satisfied, even comfortable, with the knowledge that these expectations will always fall short of being met. Instead, sharing a few key examples—a moment when you saw the world differently or a story of a surprising meal you had—can allow you to communicate some of these experiences without having to fully explain your entire journey.

One thing to remember is this: *You don't owe anyone anything*. Your decision to share your travel experience is entirely your choice. You may decide that you don't actually *want* to talk about your trip. You don't have to. At the end of the day, these experiences are yours and yours alone to remember. Whether you choose to share them with others or not is something that only you can decide. The moments you had belong to you. That's what makes solo trips so special.

Introducing Loved Ones to the "New You"

Every trip changes you in unique and different ways. Your first solo trip might stand out particularly strongly, even if it's just a week or two long. You've spent a lot of time and energy doing the work not just to go somewhere but to let yourself be affected and changed. But then you come home and it feels nearly impossible to communicate that change to the people who love you most and, at least up until now, know you best.

On the inside we'll feel different. We may feel like we have a new global identity and a new perspective that is an instrumental part of us. But there's not much on the outside that will indicate to the world how monumental those changes have been, besides maybe a nice tan or a new tattoo. Your loved ones might not even notice how changed you feel. And in fairness, how could they? They haven't gone on your journey with you. Only you will fully understand what you experienced, what you saw, and how it affected you. This might feel jarring or overwhelming. In some cases we may feel like some of our closest friends and family can no longer understand or appreciate a part of us that feels remarkably important and central to who we are, and that feels really suffocating. It may seem like these relationships are ones we should abandon or move away from, simply because that other person can no longer see this part of us that has changed so fundamentally. But just as we may have discovered and come to love new parts of ourselves, so we have an endless capacity of love for others. No single person needs to be our everything, not even our closest friends and family. They don't need to understand and serve every part of who we are.

Dr. Cate said it best: "We go abroad, and we hope that when we come back, people will see it, and they still don't. And I think we've got to stop caring about that. Instead of focusing on the other people and what they're not doing or giving us in reentry, we need to focus on ourselves. 'How did this change me? Who am I now? What do I want? What do I want my life to be like now? What am I willing to put up with? What am I not willing to put up with? Which relationships serve me? Which ones don't? What are my boundaries?'" Being really clear about those boundaries and those expectations for yourself and for others will help those relationships continue to bloom and grow, even after your return home.

Seeing my relationships in this way allowed me to understand more deeply how much our expectations of one another sometimes become self-fulfilling prophecies. If you expect someone to be a certain way, it's so much likelier they'll fit that mold because continuing a habit is the easiest route. But if you give people a little freedom, their ability to adapt may surprise you (and them). You might find that you feel a little bit freer around friends who give you the emotional space to embrace your "new" self. But you might also see old relationships in new ways, too, because you're simultaneously giving others—even people you thought you knew perfectly—the chance to express a part of themselves that may have evolved in other ways you haven't seen before. Wouldn't that make sense, anyway? After all, traveling the world as you have, you've already surprised yourself many times. The people you're close to may surprise you, too.

Sharing Bits of Your Trip

It may be difficult to find the time and the space to really express what this trip was like for you to someone you care about in a way that goes beyond a highlights reel. Here are some nice ways to "break the ice" for you both and give you the opportunity to talk about the great parts of your trip as well as the things that felt more complicated:

- Bring home a recipe and prepare a dish for friends and family that you ate while abroad. Have your guests help prep the food and tell them stories about your trip while you do it.
- Practice a new hobby or passion. If you found yourself getting really fired up about animal rights on your trip, invite a friend to go with you to the local animal shelter and use that as a way to talk about how that experience affected you abroad.
- If the place you visited has a strong immigrant community where you live, attend their events and amplify their work. Take your family out to a Haitian restaurant on New Year's Day to eat soup joumou, invite your friend to a Nowruz party, or bring your partner to an event hosted by the local Japanese bookstore. While we know travel and culture aren't just about parties and celebrations, taking your friends to a physical event could open the doors to explore your travel stories more deeply while also exposing them to some of the traditions you learned.

- Listen to music together. Download a playlist of top hits in the place you just visited, or old classics (wherever your preference lies), and listen to them with someone you care about. Maybe you'll recognize some of the songs from the TV or radio while you were traveling, or maybe you'll experience something new together.

INTRODUCING YOU TO...YOURSELF

My favorite quote of all time also happens to come from one of my most favorite people, the great poet and activist Maya Angelou:

> *I long, as does every human being, to be at home wherever I find myself.*

To me, this quote is the ultimate homage to travel. It consists of reaching an emotional place where you wholly and completely trust yourself and become a true citizen of the world. Where you can be at home with yourself wherever you are, because that home doesn't exist in any one specific location or set of coordinates. That home exists within you.

It doesn't mean that you're never uncomfortable or that you're never learning, of course. Finding home with yourself means that you welcome those feelings of discomfort because you know them like an old friend. You find them still nestled in that suitcase. But beside them, you find one other thing: A sense of global citizenship. A feeling that your home is the world. A deep and significant sense of belonging.

Finding home within yourself takes work (and if you think I've mastered it, think again). Your solo trip may have upended some of the things you thought you knew about who you are. You will have grown significantly, many times over what you will grow in a typical week or month at home. You will have spent your entire trip learning, questioning, pivoting, adjusting. Your travel muscles will have gotten quite a bit of exercise, and that might affect how you look at and think about yourself. It will feel like trying on an old shirt and noticing how it fits you differently. All those weeks at the travel gym changed your physique.

I've always felt that the true souvenirs of a trip—the things that stay with you, that take up space in your mind and heart and life—are the things that you notice about yourself and the world. They may be small things, like my discovery that I'd been using utensils wrong my entire life (apparently you're supposed to hold your fork in your nondominant hand—who knew?), or wondering why in the world I don't take regular fifteen-minute espresso breaks during the workday. But they also may be bigger things, like noticing how you're treated differently abroad than you are at home due to your gender, your neurodiversity, or your physical appearance. Or realizing that the whole way you felt about your own family relationships was off. These things that you notice likely unearthed biases you yourself had that you didn't even know you had. You may start to question yourself and why you've said or done certain things in the past. The world may be more confusing, but other things may feel clearer.

These realizations have an effect on a much more systemic level, too. You might experience another country's health-care system and realize it's way more efficient and affordable. You might be dumbfounded by how another city accommodates its wheelchair users or cares for its new parents. You might eat the most delicious local fruit picked right off a tree and start to have thoughts about your local growing systems and food supply chains at home. These discoveries may impact your life both positively and negatively. They may even become the focus of your life's work, as they did for me.

You also might not even notice any changes in yourself right away. You might have been so quick to move back into the rhythms of home that what you experienced will not even hit you until two weeks later while sitting at work and you won't know what to do with those feelings. It's funny how they will creep up on you anyway, maybe while you're paging through some documents in your cubicle or waiting in line for a large iced latte. Suddenly, you look at a very familiar menu and you're struck with a mixture of comfort and disappointment in feeling too comfortable.

For me, it often happens when I'm shopping for groceries, usually while waiting in line. Unlike my Day Zero grocery store experience when I can't often speak the local language and come across so many new food types, at home I realize I'm fluent and could literally strike up a conversation with anyone. The surrounding conversations perk up in my ears. (*It's amazing that I can understand everything without even trying*, I'll think to myself.) The poor person behind me will have no idea what he or she is in for. I tend to be very chatty in grocery stores when I return home from a trip, amazed by my own fluency in my native tongue.

The concept of returning home, for me, can be overwhelming in the best and worst ways. We adjust to a new place, and then we adjust right back to our old motions, while on the inside feeling different because we saw things and experienced things we'd never been exposed to before. We realize in those moments that we got some things right (as individuals, as a culture, as a society), and we got other things wrong. We realize how much we as humans are shaped by what's around us and how we are all flawed in our own ways. These feelings and thoughts run deep and sometimes you may feel that you need an outlet. This is where your travel journal is an ongoing gift. I recommend that you continue to use it for a few days after your trip so you can capture these moments when they creep up on you. The flight home is also an excellent time to reflect a little more deeply on your trip as a whole.

And don't forget that Day Zero doesn't work just one way! You can take advantage of its magic when you're home. Rather than diving straight back into work, school, or fast-paced life, give yourself time to just sit and be with your feelings. A day, at least. Don't tell anyone you're home yet. Don't answer your phone calls; keep your auto-responder up a bit longer. Flip through your pictures. Unpack your bags. Order that ham and pineapple pizza you've been missing. Give yourself time to sit, absorb, decompress, and write.

Journal Prompts After Returning Home

Try some of these prompts to help you process your feelings after returning home:

- Is there anything from this experience that I wish I could keep home with me, whether local ways of living, mindsets, or a way I found myself acting that was a surprise to me?

- What have I learned about this culture that made me uncomfortable? Why do I feel this way?
- Are there any moments of my life that I now see differently? Which ones?
- What will I miss the most and why?
- What do I wish my loved ones knew about me now?
- What have I learned about myself?

If this is the first time you've fallen in love with another place, you may feel the pang in your heart of knowing that you'll never be able to be in two places you love at the same time. These thoughts and feelings are part of a new chapter that is unfolding for you, a chapter that's even more colorful and exciting than you could ever imagine. You become as bewildered as Dorothy, departing her life in Kansas and suddenly experiencing Technicolor for the first time and a whole world outside her family farm. This adventure brings you to a crossroads and a choice: You can retreat, dismissing your global adventure as a memory of what happened and is now gone. You can shift, closing the door on the "old you," including the people who you believe understand only a small part of who you are. Or you can embrace the sparkle of your new global identity, which, from here on out, will add a whole new dimension to the way you see your world every day for the rest of your life.

There is one friend, of course, whom you do get to tell all your stories to. The friend who knows the nuances of all of your travel experiences—the moments when you felt confused, or wrong, or joyful. The friend who will never get tired of your memories. Whom you might have gotten to know in new ways. Outside the forces of your home environment, perhaps you even felt like you met her for the first time. Of course, that friend is you. Maybe you've never thought about yourself as your own friend before. But I hope you will now. She is the person who will accompany you on many more adventures and journeys. And when you give her a bit of space, she's actually really awesome.

In fact, when you return home, you might even feel like you miss her a little bit.

"A lot of people feel like they're failing when they come home," Dr. Cate explained to me. "When you decide to come home, you lose that identity of being really cool, and having really great pictures. Now, suddenly, you're boring like everyone else."

While your environment has contributed to making you who you are, your environment is not you. That person you may have come to love abroad (or to better understand, at least) has always been in you. After you return home, she won't have gone anywhere. There are ways that you will be able to continue to cultivate and nurture those parts of you wherever you are in the world and even at home. And in doing so, you will begin to understand what it means to be a true Wander Woman— not necessarily to constantly be on the road, packing a suitcase every four seconds. But to bring your global identity—your global life—into your everyday. To let yourself be surprised, confused, and challenged not just thousands of miles away from home but one mile away. To meet new people and relish new stories not across oceans, but across city streets, across neighborhood communities, across cultures, and even across political and social divides. To find home everywhere. That is the role of a true Wander Woman—not to always seek out more ways to travel, but to find the inherent components of a travel experience wherever you are.

WHEN YOUR HOME IS THE WORLD

I'm not sure what the moment was, exactly, when my global identity became more clear to me. It happened slowly. Over time I began to realize that who I was, was not a fixed thing; that I was constantly evolving, and learning, and growing, and adapting. There wasn't a "pre-trip Beth" and a "post-trip Beth." There was only Beth, and that person was a beautiful, flexible, constantly changing creature. Realizing that about myself allowed me to tap into some of the pleasures of travel right from home. After studying abroad in Portugal, I got a job broadcasting international radio news in Portuguese; I started working for the Portuguese embassy and eventually went back overseas. My Portuguese knowledge is what took me to São Tomé. My trip to São Tomé is what led me to create Wanderful.

I opened my windows and doors widely to see what other global experiences could happen right in my home country, and I was overwhelmed (in a good way) with the opportunities. I realized one of the most important things about travel that I want to pass along to you:

Your trip didn't change you. You changed yourself.

And in fact, some of those parts of you that feel new were probably a part of you this whole time, just a tiny spark waiting for the right combination of fuel and air to set afire.

Yes, these outside factors were an enormous part. You saw

things you didn't even know about before. You had conversations with people that changed the way you looked at issues. You tasted a *pain au chocolat* for the first time. I totally get it. But you could have done all these things and not let them change you one little bit. The act of going abroad does not make you a more wise or worldly person. It is up to you to let those experiences become part of you. To embrace the spirit of challenging and questioning your preconceptions. Of letting yourself relish finding—and embracing—the new. To make sure you never get too satisfied or comfortable. To use that power inside yourself to give others permission to seek that beautiful change inside themselves, too. To be constantly growing and evolving. That is the true meaning of travel. Whether this is your first journey or your fiftieth, my wish for you is that you find travel everywhere.

YOUR GLOBAL LIFE IS YOUR SUPERPOWER

"As a woman I have no country. As a woman my country is the whole world."

—Virginia Woolf

SOME OF YOU MAY BE FAMILIAR WITH WONDER WOMAN'S most powerful weapon: her golden lasso. You may also know that her golden lasso forces people to tell the truth. But actually, that's a gross oversimplification of what her lasso does. William Moulton Marston, Wonder Woman's creator, was a polyamorous psychologist who believed in "loving submission" (and yes, the BDSM nuances are not untrue, but that's beside the point!). In many ways, Wonder Woman's golden lasso was a physical manifestation of her ability to get people to be vulnerable with her. Wonder Woman didn't force people to tell the truth. Instead, when she used it, people suddenly felt compelled to tell her things, because they felt her compassion.

If you journey deeper into the DC Fandom wiki, you'll also find that the lasso has been used throughout the years in other ways, like "tethering hearts and minds together so various individuals could better understand one another, creating a telepathic rapport between anyone and everyone holding on to it, and enabling language translation and memory/emotion sharing."[1]

Wonder Woman's Lasso of Truth was her superpower. But that superpower wasn't about force. It was about bringing people together and helping them understand one another.

Over the months upon my return, I discovered that we Wander Women also have our own golden lassos: our global citizenship. My identity as a global citizen was something that became central to who I was. I felt like I was no longer just a member of my state or country but a member of my world. Knowing that I was part of a bigger community and a bigger ecosystem calmed me. Struggling through my own moments of self-identity allowed me to give others the freedom and grace to be who they were. Seeing ways of doing things that were new to me allowed me to imagine my own immediate world not as it was then, but as it could be. And experiencing the world so deeply on my own gave me the tools to meaningfully connect with others and to give them the ability to come together and understand one another better. My identity as a citizen of the world became my golden lasso, a core part of who I am today.

Your global life doesn't stop the moment you return home. You will find it everywhere, whether you're traveling or not. You may take opportunities to feed this global identity that you have, and you can do it in numerous ways. Here are some examples:

- Embracing short jaunts and local travel; finding new things in places you thought you already knew
- Digging into your city's or country's indigenous heritage and better understanding whose land you're standing on
- Celebrating immigrant communities, whether small local businesses or major sections of your city like Chinatown or Little Italy
- Hosting travelers in your region through communities like Wanderful or volunteering at your local hostel or international exchange program
- Taking a language class or volunteering with an ESL program
- Advocating for causes that your travels made you aware of, like animal treatment, immigration, conservation, or trans rights—and getting involved with efforts in your own community

You may find that a challenge or experience you had abroad inspires you to create something new, as it did for me. Or you may simply find that the lessons you learned from your travels made you into a more flavorful, more nuanced person on the whole. Maybe you learned to be more compassionate and to listen better to others. Maybe you found yourself less impatient or more open to little adventures. You might apply these lessons in your professional life, better understanding how to lead cross-culturally. Or maybe you just have a newfound appreciation for espresso. Though this trip may be over, the things you have taken with it—the new ways you look at yourself, your society, and the world around you—are things you will use every day. And you'll realize that the real heart of travel is not in how far you go but how much you let those experiences thrill, challenge, and change you.

You'll look out into the world and suddenly see that you're in a massive garden of self-discovery, and that first solo trip was just the first stepping stone of hundreds of gorgeous stones laid out before you; stones that curve into winding pathways, and through forests, and past the ocean. Stones that cross under the cool shade of big oak trees and the harsh sun of summer. Each stone will feel like another leap into the unknown, but they'll be more manageable now, because you'll have a fresh understanding of what you can do and what you're capable of. With each step, you'll fill your tool belt with more exciting instruments that you can use on your next adventure. And maybe, just maybe, as you hop your life from one stepping stone to the next, you'll realize the most magical part of it all: that the true destination is, in fact, the journey itself.

ACKNOWLEDGMENTS

When I first started writing this book, it was July 2016.

Professionally, it was a year I was feeling on top of the world. I had just graduated with my MBA from the Kellogg School of Management at Northwestern University, a business school experience that surrounded me with some of the most brilliant entrepreneurial minds I know. I was three years into growing my company, Wanderful, and we were starting to really feel our feet not just as a travel blog but as a global resource for women around the world. We hosted our third-annual WITS Travel Creator Summit in Irvine, California, and were honored with a citywide holiday. Marvin and I were living in Chicago, a city I will always hold close to my heart as it's where Wanderful truly blossomed.

I had started writing this book because it was the book I wish someone had given to me when I first started traveling alone. A book that would arm me with helpful information and encourage me to look realistically at the world. But also a book that would be fun. A warm hug of a book that I could have settled down with when I missed my very first solo flight and slept overnight on the cold floor of Stansted Airport outside London, faced with a world that felt so much bigger than the one I had known before. This book was a way to talk to that young person about what she was about to experience, both the expected and the unexpected parts of being a woman traveling the world.

Personally, in July 2016 I had no idea what I was in for. I was newly pregnant with my first child, Nora—but I'm pretty sure I didn't even know that yet. I settled down one day and wrote my first chapter (which eventually morphed into this book's introduction). Then I discovered I was pregnant, was thrown into the whirlwind of life as a new parent, and didn't even think to pick up this book again until four years later when I was pregnant with my second child, Zoey. Sometime before Zoey was born, the fire in me was reignited with new purpose. It became not just a book for myself fifteen years ago, but a book for my daughters—and for all daughters, of any age, who needed it. Now, I write these acknowledgments while pregnant with my third child. It seems this book has followed my journey as a parent into quite a full circle.

It's with this that I should first and foremost thank another mother who saw the need for this book and helped move it forward even when I presented her with a pitch just three weeks before giving birth: my agent, Amaryah Orenstein of GO Literary Agency (as well as the amazing Liz O'Donnell, who introduced me to her). Amaryah, this book wouldn't even be here without you. You are my book doula.

Amaryah is the person who discovered quite possibly the most perfect fit of an editor, Hannah Robinson of Grand Central Publishing. I'm not sure what magic fell upon us to bring the three of us together, but I'm sure glad it happened. With the two of you behind me, I truly felt on top of the world, and I am so grateful to you both for your patience, kindness, and willingness to ride along on my many adventures.

Hannah, I honestly don't know how you do it. You are a masterful editor who seemed to always know what I wanted to say as well as a much, much better way to say it. You have fairy-godmothered this book into the most beautiful treasure I could have ever imagined. I am endlessly in awe of your skill, and it has been an absolute gift to work with you. To the entire team at Grand Central Publishing: Thanks for making this book come to life, for your amazing marketing and design skills, and for adding this important message to your portfolio.

To the Wanderful community and most importantly the Wanderful team, thank you for believing in my vision of a global network of travel-loving women, and for supporting me with your time, your energy, and your enthusiasm. So many parts of Wanderful have consisted of "Beth's wild ideas," and I am grateful to have a community of ride-or-die women who pack their bags for them. Whether poolside in Puerto Rico, on a rooftop in Peru, or drinking mulled wine on a crisp evening in Poland, I have made some of my closest friends in this community, as I know many of you have as well. Thank you for lifting me up and for helping Wanderful grow and shine. A special thanks to some of our Wanderful OGs, including Ariel Goldberg, who has spent many hours of her life helping me hone my written voice in order to say things that matter, and to Marissa Sutera, whose belief and personal investment in me from the beginning are an enormous part of the very reason I felt like Wanderful was even possible.

To everyone who has contributed to this book to share their stories, whether or not they were included in the final edit, I am grateful for the time you took to sit down with me to bare your soul for the purpose of helping others after you. There are so many trailblazers out there in the world making travel better for all of us, whether through their content, their ideas, their businesses, or their communities, and I feel honored that so many would give me not just the time of day but a moment of their own life experience, their own deepest thoughts and feelings. Thank you to Jumoke Abdullahi, Geetika Agrawal, Kareemah Ashiru, Stacy Bias, Stacey Birch, Dr. Cate Brubaker, Carol Cabezas, Jessica Cobbs, Jessica Drucker, Pauline Frommer, Lily Girma, Montoya Hudson, Martinique Lewis, Kelley Louise, Paula Lucas, Tahina Montoya, Elena Nikolova, Zi Piggott, Kathryn Pisco, Catarina Rivera, Charlotte Simpson, Gretchen Sorin, Marlene Valle, Kayley Whalen, Elin Williams, and Justine Abigail Yu, as well as dozens of others who have inspired and challenged me. To Evelyn Hannon, who modeled a life I wanted for myself and encouraged me to find my own path with my business, thank you for being the first.

Writing a book doesn't happen in a vacuum, and I am grateful to the women who published books before me and inspired me to do the same, including Deidre Mathis, Nikki Vargas, Jen Ruiz, Pippa Biddle, and, most impactfully, Dr. Anu Taranath. Anu, you never knew this, but one time on a video call with our Wanderful book club you told us that you wrote your book *Beyond Guilt Trips* seven minutes at a time because as a busy working mother that's all you had available. That singular piece of advice was what gave me the courage and confidence to pick up *Wander Woman* again even while deep in the throes of young motherhood. I owe so much of this book to that. Thank you.

Acknowledgments

I have been afforded many opportunities in life, and I have tried to not take any of them for granted. To Wellesley College's Jennifer Thomas-Starck and the University of Coimbra's João Paulo Moreira, thank you for giving me the opportunity to study abroad and discover an important part of who I was in my mother country. To Ned Seligman, thank you for opening your world to me in São Tomé and trusting me with the reins of your most precious creation. You are missed by many across the globe. To Tim Falconer, José Antonio Galaz, and Pat Ryan, thanks for taking me under your wing through various stages of my career and helping me grow. Thank you to David Schonthal of the Zell Fellows Program, who believed in Wanderful's potential (despite the gray hairs I gave him); to Kellogg's Linda Darragh, who always encouraged me to think bigger; and to Tasha Seitz, who kept up with my progress and treated me like an equal. Thank you to Ashley Lucas, Susan Duffy, Heatherjean MacNeil, and the Babson WIN Lab for supporting my entrepreneurial journey even amid my first parenting surprises; and to the Tory Burch Foundation for connecting me to an inspiring network of women that gave me a blueprint to success. Thank you to Barbara Clarke, Wanderful's first investor; and to Dina Yuen for her endless hours of mentorship. I am indebted to you both.

To my parents, Rosanne Santos and Jack Santos, thank you for having an unshakable belief in my abilities and my independence. Now that I'm a parent, I can only imagine what went through your heads when I declared that I would be moving to a remote country I hadn't heard of to live with a man I had met once, but you never questioned my judgment (at least, not in front of me) and continued to be my ultimate support system.

You knew something about me that I didn't yet know about myself, and I hope to be the kind of parent to my children that you have been to me. I love you both.

To my "later" parents, including my stepmom, Astrid Lorentzson, and my in-laws, Gladyse Bernard and Guerrena Mathelier, thank you for your encouragement, your support, and for the hundreds of days you spent helping take care of the girls so I could get work done and continue to build a career for myself, even when there were times you probably wondered if this was a "real job." This book wouldn't be here without you giving me the gifts of time and focus to create it.

To my grandmothers, Margaret Clapis and Mary Lopes, I wish you'd both had a chance to read this book, because it is the culmination of both of your life stories. Travel affected your lives deeply in different ways, and that lifeblood continues to flow through me. I miss you both every day and think of you often.

To my children, I hope this book can be just the start of many wonderful and exciting adventures as you paddle the twists and turns of life. You are, in many ways, my reason for living. I love you so very much.

And last, to my husband, Marvin Mathelier, who has been part of this book since before it was even written (and the butt of a few of my travel jokes; thanks, babe): Thank you for believing in me and pushing me to keep going, even in moments when I had all but given up on myself. You are my biggest cheerleader, my partner in crime, and the love of my life. I love you.

RESOURCES

RESOURCES

WANDERFUL RESOURCES

So many of our travel experiences can be enhanced, and even more deeply understood, with an international community of women who have been there. That's where Wanderful comes in.

BECOME A MEMBER

As a member, you get access to more than fifty local hubs, online resources and events, and even group trips and international meetups. Plus, membership is accessible and affordable.

I invite you to join our community and be part of our global sisterhood.

Learn more at www.sheswanderful.com/join.

Follow us on social: @sheswanderful on Facebook and Instagram.

Other Wanderful Creations
WITS Travel Creator Summit

For travel content creators and industry marketers: witsummit.com; @witsummitcom on Facebook; @wanderfulcreators on Instagram

The Bessie Awards

Named after Bessie Coleman, honoring women of impact in travel: bessieawards.org

Wanderfest
The first major outdoor travel festival by and for women:
wanderfestevent.com

Women-Owned Travel Database
blog.sheswanderful.com/womenowned

READY TO SHARE YOUR STORY?

We're always looking for amazing stories and tips for traveling women on our blog. Submit yours at sheswanderful.com/write.

TRAVEL RESOURCES

It's everyone's favorite part—list time!

It would take years—centuries!—to list every helpful item to pack, every travel app that's worth checking out, and every resource to continue to expand upon your love of travel. But it *is* worth highlighting some of my most favorite businesses and items, especially ones founded, owned, or led by women, as well as non-binary and gender nonconforming folks (all of which, for your convenience, are marked with an asterisk*).

Want the most updated list possible? Check out the Women-Owned Trip Database at blog.sheswanderful.com/womenowned.

Further Reading

To continue to expand your travel mindset and teach you to think differently about our world and our industry:

- *Anu Taranath, *Beyond Guilt Trips: Mindful Travel in an Unequal World*
- *Gretchen Sorin, *Driving While Black: African American Travel and the Road to Civil Rights*
- *Pippa Biddle, *Ours to Explore: Power, Privilege, and the Paradox of Voluntourism*
- *Elizabeth Becker, *Overbooked: The Exploding Business of Travel and Tourism*

- *Jennifer B. Lee, *The Fortune Cookie Chronicles: Adventures in the World of Chinese Food*
- *Sarah Stodola, *The Last Resort: A Chronicle of Paradise, Profit, and Peril at the Beach*

Entertaining reads that also expand our global mindsets:

- *Maya Angelou, *All God's Children Need Traveling Shoes*
- *Chimananda Ngozi Adichie, *Americanah*
- *Tsh Oxenreider, *At Home in the World: Reflections on Belonging While Wandering the Globe*
- *Nikki Vargas, *Call You When I Land*
- *Liz Gilbert, *Eat, Pray, Love*
- *Yaa Gyasi, *Homegoing*
- *Malala Yousafzai, *I Am Malala*
- *Lola Akinmade, *In Every Mirror She's Black*
- *Peggielene Bartels and Eleanor Herman, *King Peggy: An American Secretary, Her Royal Destiny, and the Inspiring Story of How She Changed an African Village*
- *Azadeh Moaveni, *Lipstick Jihad: A Memoir of Growing up Iranian in America and American in Iran*
- *Hyeonseo Lee, *The Girl with Seven Names: Escape from North Korea*
- *Lisa See, *The Tea Girl of Hummingbird Lane*
- *Cheryl Strayed, *Wild*

Activities for Traveling Solo That Go Beyond Meetup.Com

Meetup.com is a great resource for finding and connecting with others when you travel alone, but there are so many other goodies worth using, too:

- *Eatwith: Join tables of foodies for meals around the world hosted by enthusiastic cooks. Think Airbnb for dinner. (Camille Rumani, cofounder)

  https://www.eatwith.com/
- *Flytographer: Hire a photographer wherever you go and get great travel pics of yourself. (Nicole Smith, founder)

  https://www.flytographer.com/
- *Remote Year: Take a year (or just a few months) traveling with a group while everyone works remotely at their day jobs. (Tue Le, CEO)

  https://www.remoteyear.com/
- *Sojrn: Take "adult study abroad" courses on topics like history in

Rome, wellness in Bali, and architecture in Barcelona. (Tara Cappel, founder)

https://www.sojrn.travel/

- *Traveling Spoon: Similar to Eatwith, including cooking classes. (Aashi Vel and Steph Lawrence, founders)
  https://www.travelingspoon.com/
- *VAWAA (Vacation with an Artist): Stay with artists around the world and learn their craft. (Geetika Agrawal, founder)
  https://vawaa.com/
- *VolunteerMatch.org: Find volunteer opportunities at home and abroad. (Judy Reilley, CEO)
  https://www.volunteermatch.org/
- *Wanderful (yay!): Find a local hub at sheswanderful.com/chapters for ongoing events, brunches, and more with travel-loving women. (Beth Santos, founder)
  https://www.sheswanderful.com
- Workaway: Use your professional skills to find meaningful work in exchange for room and board.
  https://www.workaway.info/
- *WWOOF (Worldwide Opportunities on Organic Farms): Work on organic farms around the world in exchange for room and board. (Sue Coppard, founder)
  https://wwoof.net/

Places to Stay Beyond Airbnb and Vrbo

- AutoCamp: Luxury airstreams for camping newbies.
  https://autocamp.com/
- Community Homestay Network: Stay locally throughout Nepal with the whole community hosting you.
  https://www.communityhomestay.com/
- Getaway House: Cozy off-the-grid cabins.
  https://getaway.house/
- *Golightly: Women's homesharing community. (Victoria O'Connell, founder)
  https://www.wegolightly.com
- Hostelling International: Nonprofit hostel chain that offers travel abroad scholarships.
  https://www.hiusa.org

- *Kid & Coe: Vacation rentals for families, for that moment when you bring a kiddo along. (Zoie Kingsbery Coe, founder)
  https://www.kidandcoe.com/
- *Kind Traveler: Socially conscious hotel booking platform that gives back to global causes. (Jessica Blotter, CEO and founder)
  https://www.kindtraveler.com/
- Misterbnb: LGBTQ+ friendly accommodations (despite the name, gals use it too).
  https://www.misterbandb.com/
- Outdoorsy: Peer-to-peer RV rentals (yup, Airbnb for RVs).
  https://www.outdoorsy.com/
- Trusted Housesitters: Stay in people's homes for free while pet-sitting abroad.
  https://www.trustedhousesitters.com/
- *Wanderstay Hotels: First hostel owned by an African American woman, also with a sister boutique hotel in Houston, Texas. (Deidre Mathis, founder)
  https://wanderstayhotels.com

Walking Tours and More

See the world a little differently with local guides:

- Airbnb Experiences: Activities and tours with amateur local hosts.
  https://www.Airbnb.com
- Context Travel: Small group tours around the world with scholarly experts.
  https://www.contexttravel.com/
- Free Tours by Foot: Free walking tours around the world.
  https://www.freetoursbyfoot.com
- Intrepid Urban Adventures: Walking tours, food tours, and even cooking classes. (Owned by B-Corp Intrepid Travel)
  https://www.urbanadventures.com
- *Invisible Cities: This company trains people who have experienced homelessness to give tours in cities across the UK. (Zakia Moulaoui, founder)
  https://invisible-cities.org/
- *Moonlight Experiences: Not tours per se, but queer events around the world with ticketed small group experiences. (Aisha Shaibu-Lenoir, founder)
  https://www.moonlightexperiences.com/

- Sandemans NEW Europe: Free walking tours around Europe and the Middle East.
  https://www.neweuropetours.edu
- Tours by Locals: Private tours with hand-picked guides.
  https://www.toursbylocals.com
- Walks: Small group walking tours throughout North America and Europe.
  https://www.takewalks.com/

Group Travel Opportunities

These companies offer small group trips, often focused specifically on women:

- *Around the World Beauty Tours: Group experiences centered around engaging with local beauty traditions, plus thoughtfully sourced global beauty products for sale online. (Stephanie Flor, founder)
  https://www.aroundtheworldbeautyjourneys.com/
- *Cheema's Travel: Small group culinary trips. (Rani Cheema, founder)
  https://www.cheemastravel.com/
- *Damesly: Creative retreats for professional women. (Kelly Lewis, founder)
  https://damesly.com/
- *FTLO Travel (For the Love of Travel): Modern group travel for ages twenty-five to thirty-nine; older sister company of Sojrn. (Tara Cappel, founder)
  https://www.ftlotravel.com/
- *Girl Around the Globe: Intimate group trips for women seeking off-the-beaten-path adventures. (Dominique Jackson, founder)
  https://girlaroundtheglobe.co/
- *Global Family Travels: Immersive, community-led trips. (Jennifer Spatz, founder)
  https://www.globalfamilytravels.com/
- Intrepid Women's Expeditions: Immersive all-female adventures focused on women-owned businesses and with women tour guides.
  https://www.intrepidtravel.com/us/womens-expeditions
- *Lotus Sojourns: Beyond-the-bucket-list experiences for women. (Christine Winebrenner Irick, founder)
  https://www.lotussojourns.com/

- *The Centre for GOOD Travel: Purposefully designed group trips that give back sustainably to local communities, plus capacity-building workshops. (Eliza Raymond, Shelley Bragg, Caitie Goddard, and Heidy Aspilcueta, cofounders)
https://www.good-travel.org/
- WanderRock: International small group adventures for neurodiverse young adults.
https://wanderrock.com/

Adventure- and Outdoors-Focused Women's Travel Companies

- *Adventure Women: One of the original women's adventure travel groups started in 1982. (Susan Eckert, founder)
https://www.adventurewomen.com/
- *Adventures in Good Company: Long-standing women's group adventure travel since 1999. (Marian Marbury, founder)
https://www.adventuresingoodcompany.com/
- *Explorer Chick: Hiking adventures and "SHE-nanigans" with certified guides. (Nicki Bruckmann, founder)
https://explorerchick.com/
- *Fit & Fly: Fitness-focused trips with on-hand fitness instructors. (Rebecca Garland, cofounder)
https://www.fitandflygirl.com/
- *Origin Travels: Immersive group adventures. (Britt Kasco, founder)
https://origin-travels.com/
- REI Adventures: The outdoor retailer's own brand of trips guided by women, for women.
https://www.rei.com/adventures/t/womens
- *She Moves Mountains: Backpacking and climbing retreats. (Lizzy VanPatten, founder)
https://shemovesmountains.org/
- *WHOA Travel: Energetic, soul-inspiring treks to Kilimanjaro and more. (Allison Fleece and Danielle Thornton, cofounders)
https://www.whoatravel.com/
- *Wild Women Expeditions: Playful and fun trips for nature lovers and adventure seekers. (Jennifer Haddow, owner)
https://wildwomenexpeditions.com/

Trip Planning Support

- *CityCatt: Travel journeys curated by local experts. (Lizia Santos, founder)
  https://www.citycatt.com/
- *Pack Up + Go: Leave the planning behind with a surprise trip planned for you. (Lillian Rafson, founder)
  https://www.packupgo.com/
- *Portico: Digital travel organizer. (Jacqueline Hampton, founder)
  https://portico.travel/
- *Seeker: Digital app for finding and sharing places. (Jody Vandergriff, founder)
  https://seeker.io/
- *WildBum: Curated travel guides. (Mollie Krengel, founder)
  https://wildbum.com/

Online Shopping

- *Local Purse: Virtual shopping tours of local markets around the world. (Lola Akinmade and Sara Mansouri, founders)
  https://www.localpurse.com/
- *Threads Worldwide: Shop fair trade jewelry and home goods online. (Angela Melfi, Kara Valentine, and Lindsay Murphy, cofounders)
  https://threadsworldwide.com/

Apparel and Accessories

- *Black Travel Box: Travel hair and skin essentials. (Orion Brown, founder)
  https://theblacktravelbox.com/
- *CapSoul: Trendy travel bags. (Marissa Wilson, founder)
  https://capsoulco.com/
- Clothing Arts: Pickpocket-proof pants and more.
  https://www.clothingarts.com/
- *Diane Kroe: Wearable travel fashion for a variety of body types. (Diane Kroe, founder)
  https://dianekroe.com/
- *DivaCup: Reusable menstrual cup. (Francine Chambers and Carinne Chambers-Saini, founders)
  Also see Moon Cup, Saalt Cup, and Flex for alternatives.
  https://shopdiva.com/

- *Drifted: Adventure apparel for women. (Puja Seth, founder)
  https://drifted.co/
- *Dry Fox Co: Quick dry towels that can fold into your purse. (Samantha Peck, founder)
  https://www.dryfoxco.com/
- *Flare bracelets and jewelry: Safety jewelry that instantly alerts your key contacts, the police, or both—and also looks cute. (Sara Dickhaus de Zarraga and Quinn Fitzgerald, cofounders)
  http://www.getflare.com
- *Flex-n-Fly: Flexbags minimalist travel bags. (Youmie Jean Francois, founder)
  https://theflexbags.com/
- *Lo & Sons: Smart, sustainably made bags designed by a travel-savvy mom and her two adult sons. (Helen Lo, cofounder)
  https://www.loandsons.com/
- *Ms. Jetsetter: Travel accessories and jewelry holders. (Tracey McGhee, founder)
  https://msjetsetter.com/
- *Redbudsuds: Clean hair and body products for travel. (Aubrey Miller, owner)
  https://www.redbudsuds.com/
- *Sustainable Travel and Living: Shop sustainably sourced travel products including towels, bags, skin and hair products, and more. (Lauren Zoe Smith, founder)
  https://www.sustainabletravelandliving.com/
- *The Travel Bra: Bras with secret pockets. (Dr. Annie Holden, founder)
  https://www.thetravelbra.com/
- *Thinx: Reusable period underwear. (Antonia Saint Dunbar, Miki Agrawal, and Radha Agrawal, cofounders)
  See also Knix, Saalt for alternatives.
  https://www.thinx.com/
- *Tonik Cycling: Women's cycling apparel. (Kristina Vetter, founder)
  https://www.tonikcycling.com/
- *Waypoint Goods: Infinity scarves and other travel accessories. (Caitlin Blythe, founder)
  https://waypointgoods.com/

Communities

More than just communities, many of these organizations offer online spaces, offline chapters, group trips, events, and more:

- *Black Girls Travel Too: Encouraging women of color to leave their backyards and live through travel. (Danny Rivers-Mitchell, founder) https://www.blackgirlstraveltoo.com/
- *Black Travel Alliance: Nonprofit that encourages, educates, and equips Black travel professionals in education, media, and corporate positions. (Martinique Lewis, founder) https://blacktravelalliance.org/
- *Blind Travelers' Network: Articles, discussion boards, and events for blind travelers. (Stacy Cervenka, founder) https://blindtravelersnetwork.org/
- *Brown People Camping: A social media initiative that advocates for greater diversity, equity, access, and social justice in the outdoors. (Ambreen Tariq, founder) https://www.brownpeoplecamping.com/
- *Deafinitely Wanderlust: A blog and community for Deaf travelers. (S. Marlene Valle, founder) https://deafinitelywanderlust.com/
- *Disabled Hikers: Disability community and justice in the outdoors. (Syren Nagakyrie, founder) https://www.disabledhikers.com/
- *Fat Girls Traveling: Dedicated to telling fat stories, highlighting fat bodies, and changing the landscape of travel, fashion, and lifestyle brands. (Annette Richmond, founder) https://fatgirlstraveling.com/
- *Flash Foxy: Created to empower women climbers. (Shelma Jun, founder) https://www.flashfoxy.com/
- *Girl Camper: Camper/RV community. (Janine Pettitt, founder) https://girlcamper.com/
- *Latinas Who Travel: Created to encourage and empower Latinas, women of color, and honorary Latinas. (Olga Maria, founder) https://latinaswhotravel.com/
- *Latinxhikers: Breaking down barriers in the outdoors for Latinx people. (Luz Lituma and Adriana Garcia, cofounders) https://www.latinxhikers.com/

- LGBT Outdoors: Connecting queer people with the outdoors. https://www.lgbtoutdoors.com/
- *Love Her Wild: UK-based nonprofit women's adventure community. (Bex Band, founder) https://www.loveherwild.com/
- *Melanin Base Camp: Increasing the visibility of outdoorsy Black, indigenous, people of color, as well as their representation in the media and stories. (Danielle Williams, founder) https://www.melaninbasecamp.com/
- *Native Women's Wilderness: For Native women to celebrate the wilderness of their native lands. (Jaylyn Gough, founder) https://www.nativewomenswilderness.org/
- *Outdoor Afro: Celebrates and inspires Black connections and leadership in nature. (Rue Mapp, founder) https://outdoorafro.org/
- *Pink Coconuts: Events and community for LGBTQ people around the world. (Zi Piggott, founder) https://pinkcoconuts.com/
- *Plus Size Travel Too: Providing information and community for plus-size travelers. (Kirsty Leanne, founder) https://www.plussizetraveltoo.com/
- *Sisters on the Fly: Outdoors lovers, fly fishers, campers, and more. (Maurrie Sussman and Becky Clarke, founders) sistersonthefly.com
- *SurfearNEGRA: Nonprofit bringing cultural and gender diversity to the sport of surf. (GiGi Lucas, founder) https://www.surfearnegra.com/
- *Teach with Love Global: Global trips for international educators. (Taína Benitez, founder) https://www.teachwithlove.com/
- *Unlikely Hikers: Advocates for body inclusivity and anti-racism in the outdoors. (Jenny Bruso, founder) https://unlikelyhikers.org/
- Venture Out Project: Backpacking and wilderness trips for the queer and transgender community. https://www.ventureoutproject.com/

Informative Resources for Conscious Travelers

- *Jet-Set Offset: Automatically donate one cent per mile to your favorite environmental cause. (Anna Ford and Erica Eliot, cofounders)
  https://jetsetoffset.com/
- Native Land Digital: Know the indigenous name of your homeland and the tribes that originated there.
  https://native-land.ca
- *RISE Travel Institute: Courses for conscious travelers. (Vincie Ho, founder)
  https://www.risetravelinstitute.org/

A Few Helpful Apps

- AllTrails: Find hiking and running paths wherever you go.
  https://www.alltrails.com/
- *bSafe: Safety app that triggers emergency calls. (Charlen Larsen, cofounder)
  https://www.getbsafe.com/
- *EMME: Birth control reminder app (and it adjusts to time zones). (Amanda French and Janene Fuerch, cofounders)
  https://emme.com/
- FlightAware: Check the status of your flight.
  https://flightaware.com/
- HappyCow: Find vegan and vegetarian food abroad.
  https://www.happycow.net/
- Luggage Hero: Luggage storage around the world.
  See Stasher also.
  https://luggagehero.com/; https://stasher.com/
- PackPoint: Helps you decide what to pack based on location, weather, and so on.
  https://www.packpnt.com/

Resources for Preparation

- STEP (Smart Traveler Enrollment Program).
  https://step.state.gov/STEP/Index.aspx
- Centers for Disease Control: Assessments of your upcoming destination.
  https://wwwnc.cdc.gov/travel/

- For American Citizens: Find your nearest US embassy.
  http://www.usembassy.gov/
- Refuge Restrooms: Open-source website that has listings of single-stall
  and gender-inclusive restrooms around the United States and Europe.
  https://www.refugerestrooms.org/
- International Association for Medical Assistance to Travelers.
  https://www.iamat.org/
- National Center for Transgender Equality: Know your rights about
  airports, passports, and more.
  https://transequality.org/know-your-rights

In Case of Emergency

- Crisis Text Line (US only).
  https://www.crisistextline.org/
- Global Rescue: Travel assistance, health support, and medical evacuation.
  https://www.globalrescue.com/
- National Human Trafficking Hotline.
  http://humantraffickinghotline.org/; 1 (888) 373-7888
- OutRight Action International: Human rights advocacy on behalf of
  people who experience discrimination or abuse on the basis of their
  actual or perceived sexual orientation, gender identity, or expression.
  https://outrightinternational.org/
- *Pathways to Safety International: For victims of interpersonal and
  gender-based violence abroad.
  https://pathwaystosafety.org/
- RAINN National Sexual Assault Hotline.
  1-800-656-4673; or online chat: https://hotline.rainn.org/
- Sexual Assault Support and Help for Americans Abroad (SASHAA)
  hotline and online chat.
  https://sashaa.org/
- Wikipedia list of emergency contraceptives' availability by country.
  https://en.wikipedia.org/wiki/Emergency_contraceptive_availability
  _by_country

NOTES

Introduction: So You Want to Travel

1. Lacey Pfalz, "Women Uplift Travel: Why Women Are So Integral to the Industry," *TravelPulse*, March 7, 2023. https://www.travelpulse.com/voices/opinions/women-uplift-travel-why-women-are-so-integral-to-the-industry.

2. Candida Moss, "One of Christianity's First Female Pilgrims Was a Badass," *The Daily Beast*, November 23, 2018. https://www.thedailybeast.com/egeria-one-of-christianitys-first-female-pilgrims-was-a-badass.

Chapter One

1. Sally French, "The No. 1 Reason Some People Aren't Traveling This Year," *NerdWallet*, March 7, 2023. https://www.nerdwallet.com/article/travel/why-people-arent-traveling-2023#:~:text=Going%20surveyed%20thousands%20of%20its,work%20or%20school%3A%2026%25.

2. World Bank Group, "Nearly Half the World Lives on Less than $5.50 a Day," World Bank, October 17, 2018. https://www.worldbank.org/en/news/press-release/2018/10/17/nearly-half-the-world-lives-on-less-than-550-a-day.

3. World Bank, "Unlocking Supply and Overcoming Hesitancy: Eastern and Southern Africa's COVID-19 Vaccination Journey," June 30, 2022. https://www.worldbank.org/en/news/immersive-story/2022/06/30/unlocking-supply-and-overcoming-hesitancy-eastern-and-southern-africa-s-covid-19-vaccination-journey.

Chapter Two

1. Statista, "Desktop Operating System Market Share 2013–2023" |

Statista, September 4, 2023. https://www.statista.com/statistics/218089/global-market-share-of-windows-7/#:~:text=Microsoft's%20Windows%20was%20the%20dominant,a%20fifth%20of%20the%20market.

2. Lacey Pfalz, "Women Uplift Travel: Why Women Are So Integral to the Industry," *TravelPulse*, March 7, 2023.

3. Whizy Kim, with photographs by Franey Miller, "Why Women Are Being Disproportionately Impacted by Coronavirus Job Losses," *Refinery29*, April 9, 2020.

4. "Solo Traveler Annual Survey | Survey Results: A Closer Look at Solo Travelers | *Overseas Adventure Travel*," www.oattravel.com, November 24, 2020. https://www.oattravel.com/community/the-inside-scoop/the-buzz/solo-traveler-survey-results.

5. Kristin Mariano, "Muslim Women Love to Travel Solo and It's Worth USD 80 Billion," *Travel Daily*, November 6, 2019. https://www.traveldailymedia.com/muslim-women-love-to-travel-solo-and-its-worth-usd-80-billion/.

6. Andrea Smith, "Women over 50 Are Leading the Solo Travel Boom in the UK," *Lonely Planet*, January 15, 2018. https://www.lonelyplanet.com/news/women-over-50-solo-travel.

7. Matt Turner, "Stats: Black U.S. Leisure Travelers Spent $109.4 Billion in 2019," *Travel Agent Central*, November 19, 2020. https://www.travelagentcentral.com/your-business/stats-black-u-s-leisure-travelers-spent-109-4-billion-2019.

8. Statista Research Department, "Solo Holiday Travel by Age 2018 Survey," *Statista*, March 31, 2022. https://www.statista.com/statistics/934203/solo-holiday-travel-by-age-united-kingdom-uk/.

9. Condor Ferries, "Https://Www.Condorferries.Co.Uk/Solo-Travel-Statistics," n.d. https://www.condorferries.co.uk/solo-travel-statistics.

Chapter Three

1. Wanderful Study, conducted 2014.

2. Sebnem Arsu and Marc Santora, "Vacationing Staten Island Woman Found Dead in Turkey," *The New York Times*, February 2, 2013. https://www.nytimes.com/2013/02/03/nyregion/vacationing-staten-island-woman-found-dead-in-turkey.html.

3. Steve Hendershot, "All Big Cities Have a Violence Problem. Chicago's Is Different," *Crain's Chicago Business*, October 14, 2022. https://

www.chicagobusiness.com/crains-forum-safer-chicago/chicago-violence
-problem-debate-safety-inequality.

4. Steve Hendershot, "All Big Cities Have a Violence Problem. Chicago's Is Different," *Crain's Chicago Business*, October 14,
2022. https://www.chicagobusiness.com/crains-forum-safer-chicago
/chicago-violence-problem-debate-safety-inequality.

5. Steve Hendershot, "All Big Cities Have a Violence Problem. Chicago's Is Different," *Crain's Chicago Business*, October 14, 2022. https://
www.chicagobusiness.com/crains-forum-safer-chicago/chicago-violence
-problem-debate-safety-inequality.

Chapter Six

1. UNEP–UN Environment Programme, "Tourism," n.d. https://
www.unep.org/explore-topics/resource-efficiency/what-we-do/responsible
-industry/tourism.

2. "Global Estimates of Modern Slavery: Forced Labour and Forced
Marriage," 2017, Geneva: International Labour Organization and Walk
Free Foundation. https://www.ilo.org/wcmsp5/groups/public/—dgreports/
—dcomm/documents/publication/wcms_575479.pdf.

3. Hrvoje Carić, "Cruising Tourism Environmental Impacts: Case
Study of Dubrovnik, Croatia," *Journal of Coastal Research*, 2011, 104–13,
https://www.jstor.org/stable/41510783?mag=the-high-environmental-costs
-of-cruise-ships&seq=7 and https://www.facebook.com/macdja; "The High
Environmental Costs of Cruise Ships," *JSTOR Daily*, July 2019, https://daily.
jstor.org/the-high-environmental-costs-of-cruise-ships/.

4. UN World Tourism Organization, "UN Report Underscores Importance of Tourism for Economic Recovery in 2022." Accessed September
23, 2023. https://www.unwto.org/news/un-report-underscores-importance
-of-tourism-for-economic-recovery-in-2022.

5. Sandra Zapata-Aguirre and Juan Gabriel Brida, "The Impacts of the
Cruise Industry on Tourism Destinations," November 9, 2008. https://
papers.ssrn.com/sol3/papers.cfm?abstract_id=1298403.

6. Allied Market Research, "Sustainable Tourism Market Size, Share,
Growth, Forecast 2032," n.d. https://www.alliedmarketresearch.com
/sustainable-tourism-market-A06549.

7. Expedia Group Media Solutions, "Travelers' Interest in Sustainable
Tourism Options Increases," *Hospitality Net*, April 25, 2023. https://www
.hospitalitynet.org/news/4116067.html.

8. Libby Wells, "Average Cost of a Vacation: Transportation, Food, Entertainment," Bankrate, November 28, 2021. https://www.bankrate.com /banking/cost-of-vacation/.

9. Vicki Levy, "2020 Travel Trends," *AARP 2020 Travel Trends*, January. https://doi.org/10.26419/res.00359.001.

10. Irmgard Bauer, "More Harm Than Good? The Questionable Ethics of Medical Volunteering and International Student Placements," *Tropical Diseases, Travel Medicine and Vaccines* 3, no. 1 (March 6, 2017). https://doi .org/10.1186/s40794-017-0048-y.

11. BBC News, "Climate Change: Should You Fly, Drive or Take the Train?," *BBC News*, August 23, 2019. https://www.bbc.com/news/science -environment-49349566.

12. International Energy Agency, "After Steep Drop in Early 2020, Global Carbon Dioxide Emissions Have Rebounded Strongly— News," IEA, March 2, 2021. https://www.iea.org/news/after-steep-drop -in-early-2020-global-carbon-dioxide-emissions-have-rebounded -strongly.

13. Mark Spalding, Lauretta Burke, and Alan Fyall, "Covid-19: Implications for Nature and Tourism," *Anatolia*, July, 1–2. https://doi.org/10.1080 /13032917.2020.1791524.

14. "2023 Adventure Travel Industry Snapshot | Adventure Travel Trade Association," n.d. https://learn.adventuretravel.biz/research/2023 -adventure-travel-industry-snapshot.

15. Joanna Simmons, "Overtourism in Venice from Responsible Travel," Responsibletravel.com, 2017. https://www.responsibletravel.com/copy /overtourism-in-venice.

16. Rosie Bell, "Can Travel Cure Bias?" *Lonely Planet*, August 9, 2020. https://www.lonelyplanet.com/articles/benefits-of-travel.

17. Mark "Gooch" Noguchi, "The History Behind Why Hawaiians Are Obsessed with Spam," *Vice*, January 8, 2016, accessed August 1, 2023. https://www.vice.com/en/article/mgx7yx/why-hawaiians-are-utterly -obsessed-with-spam.

18. Marco Antonio Robledo and Julio Batle, "Transformational Tourism as a Hero's Journey," *Current Issues in Tourism* 20, no. 16 (2015): 1736–48. https://doi.org/10.1080/13683500.2015.1054270.

19. Megan O'Grady, "Why Are There So Few Monuments That Successfully Depict Women?" *New York Times*, February 18, 2021. https://www .nytimes.com/2021/02/18/t-magazine/female-monuments-women.html.

Chapter Eight

1. Tara Sophia Mohr, "Why Women Don't Apply for Jobs Unless They're 100% Qualified," *Harvard Business Review*, November 2, 2021. https://hbr.org/2014/08/why-women-dont-apply-for-jobs-unless-theyre-100-qualified.

2. Priceline.com, "New Survey from Priceline.Com Unveils Travel Is Number One Mood Booster for Americans," *PR Newswire*, June 29, 2018. https://www.prnewswire.com/news-releases/new-survey-from-pricelinecom-unveils-travel-is-number-one-mood-booster-for-americans-300285839.html.

3. Karl A. Pillemer, "Living a Life Without (Major) Regrets," *Huff-Post* (blog), November 10, 2016. https://www.huffpost.com/entry/living-life-without-regrets_b_8459396.

Chapter Ten

1. "Amazon.Com: Customer Reviews: BIC Cristal For Her Ball Pen, 1.0mm, Black, 16ct (MSLP16-Blk)," n.d. https://www.amazon.com/BIC-Cristal-1-0mm-Black-MSLP16-Blk/product-reviews/B004F9QBE6.

Epilogue

1. "Lasso of Truth," n.d., DC Database, accessed April 1, 2023. https://dc.fandom.com/wiki/Lasso_of_Truth#cite_note-6.

ABOUT THE AUTHOR

Beth Santos is the founder and CEO of Wanderful, a global women's travel community. She is also the driving force behind the WITS Travel Creator Summit, as well as the Bessie Awards, which honor women of impact in travel, and Wanderfest, the first major outdoor travel festival by and for women. Regularly recognized as a changemaker in the travel industry, Beth was named godmother of the *Azamara Onward* cruise ship in 2022 and strives to amplify underrepresented voices and tell women's stories through her work as a speaker, industry consultant, and small business coach. She is a graduate of Wellesley College and Northwestern University's Kellogg School of Management, and when she's not traveling the world, she can be found exploring her home city of Boston with her husband and children.